The Boehm Journey to Ching=te=Chen, China, Birthplace of Porcelain

by Frank J. Cosentino

About the Author:

Frank J. Cosentino joined Edward Marshall Boehm, Inc. early in 1959 as executive assistant to Mr. and Mrs. Boehm. In 1960 he authored the book *"Boehm's Birds — The Porcelain Art of Edward Marshall Boehm."* His second book, *"Edward Marshall Boehm 1913-1969,"* was released in the Fall of 1970. Following *"The Boehm Journey to Ching-te-Chen, China, Birthplace of Porcelain,"* first printed in 1976, his fourth book was published in 1978, *"The Boehm Journey to Egypt, Land of Tutankhamun."* Few books about a ceramic studio or artist have been written by a person who has been both an active member of the firm and a friend and close associate of the founders.

In addition to his involvement in all aspects of the Boehm experience, Mr. Cosentino travels extensively, presenting lecture programs and exhibitions. He is now president of Edward Marshall Boehm, Inc. and of its subsidiaries, Boehm of Malvern England Limited and Boehm of Llandow Wales.

Photography:

Travel photos by Maurice Eyeington.
Porcelain still photography by Mills Studio, Philadelphia, Pa.

Library of Congress Catalog Card Number: 76-50476
ISBN 0-918096-01-4

Edward Marshall Boehm, Inc., Trenton, New Jersey 08638

Second Printing — 1984

Contents

Acknowledgments

THIS REPORT of "The Boehm Journey to Ching-te-Chen, China, Birthplace of Porcelain" is in the form of a daily narrative. Each morning and night of our visit, which spanned the time period of November 29 to December 19, 1974, I expanded the copious notes taken through each exciting day. The intention was to capture as much of the flavor and detail as possible and the enthusiastic reactions and appraisals of our threesome (Mrs. Edward Marshall Boehm, Maurice Eyeington and myself) during the stimulating, pleasant hours spent together on our three-week journey.

Special thanks are due Mrs. Boehm for allowing me to accompany her and Maurice on the China trip; our many friends at The Liaison Office of the People's Republic of China in Washington, D.C. for making the trip possible and for their important assistance in all arrangements; members of The Chinese People's Association for Friendship with Foreign Countries, our host organization, who greeted us at every stop and who helped make our visits pleasant and comfortable; our two Chinese interpreters and companions who traveled everywhere with us and gave us constant care and friendship; artists and craftsmen of the outstanding ceramic factories we visited, all of whom opened their methods and techniques, as well as their hearts, to us; and to all of our colleagues in our American and English studios for their support and artistic contributions which really made the trip possible in the first place.

F. J. Cosentino, *President*
Edward Marshall Boehm, Inc.

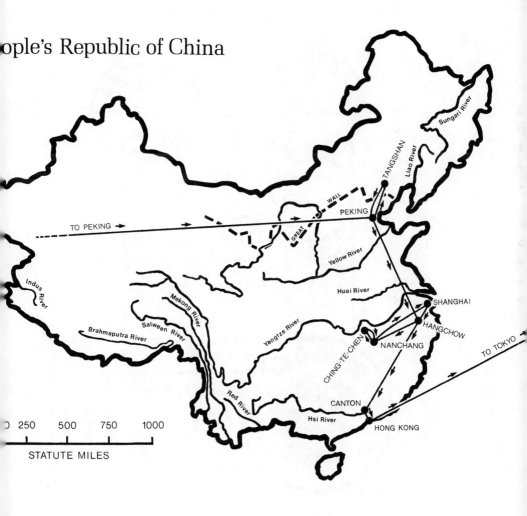

ople's Republic of China

250 500 750 1000

STATUTE MILES

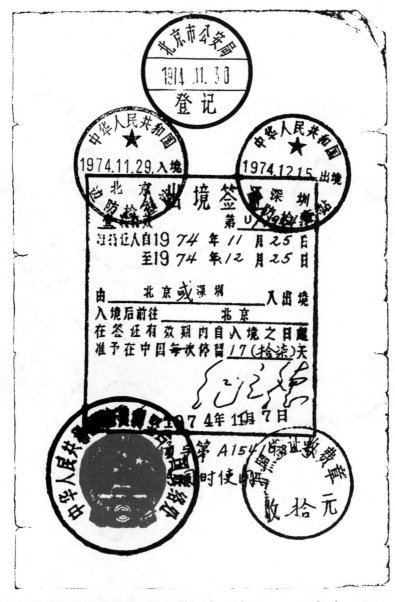

Mrs. Helen F. Boehm's visa to China, her ticket to a two-week adventure.

CHAPTER I

The "Birds of Peace" and the Start of an Adventure

It is between 2:00 and 3:00 in the morning of November 29, 1974. We've just passed over Teheran. The fact that we're really on our way to China finally is sinking in. What has been professional aplomb has quickly deteriorated to light-headed giddiness fueled by a couple of good bottles of Grand Cru burgundy.

There are three of us. Mrs. Edward Marshall Boehm, Maurice Eyeington, our head artist, and I, Frank Cosentino. We've worked together a long time. I joined the firm in Trenton, New Jersey in February 1959; Maurice about a year later. We're good friends and part of a good team.

Helen Boehm is the spirit behind it all. Six years ago her husband, Edward Marshall Boehm, world-known porcelain artist, died suddenly, leaving her with awesome responsibilities in addition to those she had always assumed as his business partner. Certainly she could have walked away from the experience and never looked back. Instead, in the face of considerable doubt and adversity, she kept the porcelain studio group together. She is talented, courageous, a spontaneous open-ended idea; a catalyst who is able to bring together people of diverse skills and personalities through her creativity and enthusiasm.

Since 1969 Mrs. Boehm has led a team which has expanded the Trenton studio, opened two outstanding porcelain studios in England (a first for American art and business) and introduced new collections in the finest porcelain media. Now represented in seventy-three museums and institutions around the world, the

1

name Boehm in fine porcelain stands comfortably alongside
Meissen, Sèvres, Chelsea, Ching-te-Chen and other great names
of history.

Lincolnesque Maurice Eyeington, six-feet-six inches tall,
gaunt, with a baronial mustache, always is impeccably dressed
and mannered. Born in Yorkshire, England, he was educated
and honed in his skills at the London Academy of Arts. For nine
years his hands and mind were one with Edward Boehm's. Their
relationship was at the highest professional level from the day
they met—cooperative, peaceful, born of a deep mutual respect.
Maurice bears the weighty responsibility of head artist of our
porcelain studios.

I'm a member of the support cast, whom good fortune introduced to Edward and Helen Boehm early in their venture at a
time when they first realized the need for an administrative assistant. From that first meeting I was full of admiration for this
remarkable couple and their purpose.

My role on this trip is that of reporter and historian. In addition to being our photographer, Maurice will help us study and
appraise the porcelain art we see in the Chinese porcelain studios
we hope to visit; and if the opportunities arise, he'll get his hands
into the clay and trade off techniques with the Chinese artists and
craftsmen. Mrs. Boehm is the ambassador. She will provide the
charm, grace and promotional input. Wherever she goes we'll
all gain an added measure of friendship and respect from the
Chinese.

We depart New York at 7:00 p.m. November 26 via Air
France, Flight 070, arriving in Paris the following morning.
Where could one make a better break in the trip? We rest over-
night at the excellent Hotel Plaza Atheneé, then board Air France
Flight 078 at 5:30 p.m. on the 28th. The route we are taking to
China and back is the same one made famous by Dr. Henry
Kissinger on his historic first visit three years ago. We were ad-
vised of this by the Liaison Office of the People's Republic of
China in Washington, D.C. From Paris we are flying over Basel,

Munich, Salzburg, Zagreb, Belgrade, Sofija, Istanbul, Ankara, Teheran and we make our one and only fueling stop in Karachi at the end of seven hours.

If we were asked to say a word about Air France, it would have to be "outstanding." Given slight advance information about our trip and the porcelain art pieces we were carrying for presentation in China, they far exceeded the levels of courtesy and care we had hoped for. At J.F.K. in New York they met us, gave us a private room, had their press photographer on hand for pictures and releases, and found safe locations on board for our handcarried cases.

In Paris we were met by a gracious young lady on the staff of "Meet the French," an agency of the government-owned airlines, who helped us in and out of customs and drove us to and from the Hotel Plaza Atheneé.

On Flight 078 from Paris the airline personnel continue their kindness. We are given two seats for our precious porcelain cargo. Just thirty-one seats are filled on the Boeing 707.

The food from New York to Paris is good; from Paris to Karachi it is superb. We've just finished a dinner of Ballotine of Duck "en voliere," stuffed Sea Bass with aromatic herbs, Roast Filet of Beef "Parisienne;" Bottom of Artichoke "Favorite," Pilau Rice, Season Salad, Selection of French Cheeses, Pastry (chocolate mocha cake), Fresh Fruit, good coffee and liqueurs.

We will lose four hours to Karachi, arriving there at 5:30 a.m. November 29. We'll lose another three enroute to Peking, arriving there at about 3.30 p.m. Total time loss from New York will be thirteen hours. For the first time in our years of traveling we will have dinner, breakfast and lunch on the same plane. We're anticipating the last two.

Mrs. Boehm especially was looking forward to this flight. She conjured up all sorts of misty characters associated with movies like *Casablanca* and the *Orient Express*. Too bad we didn't stop in Istanbul. As it turned out, if anyone aboard appeared out of the ordinary, it probably was our "troika" lugging its strange cargo. Even Karachi airport was a disappointment in this regard. First thing we saw was a bar top filled with Coca Cola, then the usual souvenir and duty-free shops. And everyone spoke English.

We are often asked how our trip to China was arranged and the reasons for it. It's a long story, but worth telling. Ever since the presidency of the late Harry Truman, Mr. Boehm and his colleagues received from the White House and State Department commissions to provide porcelain sculptures for use as gifts by our first families and other principal U.S. dignitaries. The most active were former President and Mrs. Richard Nixon. From the time of his vice-presidency Mr. Nixon knew Edward and Helen Boehm and admired the work of the Trenton Studio. In October of 1968, just prior to the November election, Mrs. Boehm and I met Mr. and Mrs. Nixon at a special New York showing of the late President Eisenhower's memorabilia and paintings. After a pleasant chat Mr. Nixon said to Mrs. Boehm, "When we get into the White House we'll look forward to calling on Mr. Boehm for some of our important gifts."

Unfortunately Mr. Boehm died eight days after the January 21 inauguration of Mr. Nixon; but the President remained true to his word. One week later he called on Mrs. Boehm to provide eight important porcelain sculptures for his NATO trip to Europe in February and early March 1969. And he continued to look to us for gifts until he left office. On both his China and Russia trips he used a great number of Boehm sculptures.

The most important was his gift of a pair of life-size porcelain "Mute Swans" to Chairman Mao Tse-tung and the people of the People's Republic of China in February 1972 (*see color plate*). Our Trenton artists and craftsmen worked on the sculpture for almost two years before the first pair was successfully cast, assembled and fired. Just in time for China.

Of course the Swans were not originally aimed at the China trip. We began the sculpture a year and a half before the historic

journey was announced. The idea for them, however, did origi-
nate in a discussion between President Nixon and Mrs. Boehm
at the White House September 14, 1969. Mrs. Boehm had presented an important collection of porcelains to the White House
in honor of her deceased husband. President and Mrs. Nixon
were on hand to officially accept the gift from her. The collection was placed in the Oval Room at the request of the president, always to remain the property of the White House. (This
was also at the request of the president. Prior presidents and
first ladies took their Boehm birds with them when they left the
White House.)

During the dedication some of the press corps were present
and one reporter churlishly asked President Nixon if the collection included a hawk and a dove. Slightly miffed at this,
the president shot back, "No it doesn't and I'm glad. I'm rather
sick of hawks and doves." Whatever moved her to speak at this
point she'll never know, but Mrs. Boehm boldly spoke up and
said "They are kind of worn out symbols, especially the dove.
Mr. President, why don't we name a new bird of peace for the
world?"

Never suspecting what creative forces he was unleashing, the
president replied, "That's a good idea, Mrs. Boehm. Why don't
you undertake the project?" The enormity and complexity of
such an undertaking would have been quickly put out of mind by
most of us. How could one be serious about attempting to replace
the dove as a world symbol of peace? But not Helen Boehm. On
her way home from Washington she was already mapping out
her plans. She would write immediately to all of her late husband's ornithological friends around the world, advise them of
her conversation with the president and solicit their opinions of
a new bird of peace symbol to replace the dove.

The ornithologists and aviculturists eagerly gave their coun-
sel. Who knew it would be a bird among the largest of all species,
the "Mute Swan"? But this was the consensus. The Mute is found
all over the world, is known as the most tranquil of swans, has a

graceful S-curve neck, mates for life, is protective and solicitous of its family and, in fables similar to the "Swan Maiden," appears in the mythologies and folklores of most of the world's people. Obviously a good choice.

And how to realize this new image? How to translate it into a vehicle that would move millions to understand its message? Through art, of course! By recreating in porcelain, in life size, these beautiful birds. Needless to say, all of us at the studio were stunned at the prospect. Few pieces so large and so bold ever have been attempted in high-fire porcelain. But the challenge was taken and we were successful. The eventual selection of the Swans as the gift to China, the birthplace of porcelain, was a meaningful and natural result. Starting from a bold idea born in the mind of their chairman, Helen Boehm, a small group of artists and craftsmen created, through their art, a new expression of hope for peace in the world.

Along with the Swans and other Boehm porcelains, President Nixon presented copies of our book *Edward Marshall Boehm, 1913–1969* to the Chinese dignitaries, some of whom, we later were to learn, read them before being assigned in late April 1973 to their new liaison office in Washington, D.C. The first contact we had with liaison officials came quite unexpectedly early in May of the same year, 1973. On May 4, 5 and 6 we planned an ambitious and gala series of events in Washington attended by approximately 600 guests comprised of Boehm patrons, friends and appointed Boehm gallery representatives. The weekend consisted of a dedication by Mrs. Dwight D. Eisenhower to the John F. Kennedy Center for the Performing Arts of a collection of 125 Boehm porcelain sculptures (which were placed in the Eisenhower Reception Room). The collection was given jointly by the Oliver H. Delchamps families of Mobile, Alabama and the Samuel S. Lombardos of Jacksonville, Florida. There also were two nights of opera and dinner at the Center and the unveiling of our new porcelain collection for 1973.

During the busy weekend Mrs. Boehm conceived another

brilliant idea. She knew the delegation of the People's Republic of China had arrived in Washington only a week before and was busily engaged in house-hunting and in learning about our capital city. She reasoned that they probably had a bureaucratic week and might be interested in something lighter as a change of pace, porcelain art for example. Through a good friend, a host for the Chinese (and an aide to Dr. Kissinger), an invitation was extended for the delegation to view the new Boehm porcelain collections on display at the Madison Hotel. At about midnight of the day, May 5, Mrs. Boehm received a call confirming that the delegation would arrive at the Madison at 10:30 the following morning, May 6.

The leader of the delegation was Mr. Han Hsu, Deputy Chief of the Liaison Office. He was accompanied by seven colleagues. It was fortuitous that Mr. Han Hsu was very much aware of the Mute Swans sculpture and had received and read our book during President Nixon's China visit. He was well versed on our porcelains as well as others, and he and his staff thoroughly enjoyed the collection. We later learned that they stayed so long (close to an hour) that they needed to readjust their schedule for the day.

Because of security, only Mrs. Boehm greeted the delegation and presented the collection. After perusing the Madison's excellent menu, she had selected chilled fresh orange juice for her guests. Remembering the procedure used by our President and Chou En-lai, she constantly offered toasts, clicked glasses all around, and added a few gestures of her own.

Mr. Han Hsu and his colleagues were charmed by their gracious, effervescent hostess and obviously were moved by the excellence of the porcelain sculptures. Just prior to departing he presented Mrs. Boehm with a beautiful pair of carved Chinese lacquer vases. Spontaneously, she returned the gesture by giving each of the delegation one of a set of eight service plates with bird and flower designs. The guests accepted them on behalf of The People's Republic of China's Mission to Washington.

11th July, 1973

Dear Mrs. Boehm,

Your letter dated 30th May, 1973 addressed
to Mr. Han Hsu, the Deputy Chief of the Liaison
Office, has been received. Appreciating your wish
to take a collection of your beautiful porcelains
for a tour of China, Mr. Han promptly conveyed it
to the department concerned in Peking. He has not
written you because he was waiting for a reply from
Peking. Now a reply from the said department has
recently come and Mr. Han has asked me to write
you this letter.

The said department would like to consider
the possibility of arranging your tour of China in
the latter half of the year 1974; because due to
their busy programme, they find it difficult to
arrange it during this year and the first half of
next year.

I would be very grateful if you could let
me know your plans for your tour of China and the
number of porcelains you would like to take with
you, and if you could send me the photographs of
your exhibits and other related materials, so that
I could pass them on to Peking for their consideration.

With best regards,

Yours sincerely,

(Hsieh Chi-mei)
Official (Counsellor) of the
Liaison Office of the Peoples's
Republic of China in the United
States of America

CHAPTER II

The Invitation to Visit China

AFTER THE VISIT with the Chinese delegation, several good friends suggested that we consider a future visit to China in view of the evolving relationships and the common expression of our porcelain art forms. A new seed was planted. Mrs. Boehm carefully drafted a letter to Mr. Han Hsu on May 30, 1973. She thanked him and his associates for visiting the collection and for the handsome vases. The key points of the letter dealt with the magnificent Chinese history of porcelain and Mrs. Boehm asked if they would be interested in a traveling exhibition of Boehm sculptures to the major cities of the People's Republic of China sponsored and presented by herself. In her letter Mrs. Boehm wrote, "I was delighted with your comments and compliments about our collection. The highest form of praise naturally comes from those who originated the subject of praise; and certainly we recognize, and have learned from, the great tradition your people have in the making of fine porcelain."

Mrs. Boehm received an encouraging reply July 11 from Mr. Hsieh Chi-mei, Official Counsellor of the Liaison Office, in which he said Mr. Han had promptly conveyed Mrs. Boehm's letter "to the department concerned in Peking." The letter mentioned the possibility of a tour of China in the latter half of 1974. Mr. Hsieh closed by requesting our plans for a tour of China and a detailed collection of photographs, catalogs and any other relevant materials. Mrs. Boehm's response included a suggested itinerary for the traveling exhibition with dates and a great volume of supporting materials.

There was a rather long delay before another reply. We con-

9

sidered writing again but were concerned with the risk of presumption. We contacted our friends at the State Department and asked their advice. We learned that Mr. Hsieh Chi-mei was not often at the Liaison Office and it was suggested we address another letter, with copies of all prior correspondence, to Mr. Tsien Ta-yung, which we did on December 19, 1973.

After other correspondence, we received early in June 1974 the letter we were waiting for, written by Counsellor Hsieh Chi-mei:

THE LIAISON OFFICE OF THE PEOPLE'S REPUBLIC OF CHINA

2300 Conn. Ave.,N.W.
Washington, D.C. 20008

June 3, 1974

Dear Mrs. Boehm,

Your letter dated May 21, 1974 addressed to Mr. Tsien Ta-yung has been received.

I am glad to let you know that we have just received a reply from the organization concerned in Peking with regard to your wish to visit China. They have asked us to inform you that they extend their welcome to you and invite you to visit China for two weeks during this winter or next spring; and the expenses for your visit within China will be met by your host, while you pay your own way from the U.S.A. to China and from China back to the U.S.A. The said organization also express their regret at being unable to arrange your suggested exhibition as they have too busy a program. They hope you would understand.

I shall be very happy to hear from you about your visit to China.

With best wishes,

Yours sincerely,

谢 启 美

Hsieh Chi-mei
Official (Counsellor)

To the People of
the People's Republic of China
from
the Edward Marshall Boehm
Artists and Craftsmen
of the United States of America
December 1974

In friendship, gratitude and respect
for the enormous contributions of the
nese people to the honored art of Porcelain.
Presented on the visit to China
of Mrs. Edward Marshall Boehm
and her studio colleagues
Frank Cosentino and Mr. Maurice Eyeington.

All Boehm Panda Cubs bear the inscription (*left*) which appeared
on the original sculptures presented in China.

Immediately following this Mrs. Boehm received a telephone
call from Mr. Chang Chi-hsiang of the Liaison Office. He stated
he would assist in arranging the trip plans with us and asked for
a suggested itinerary, specific dates for the visit and the number
of people in the party. Mrs. Boehm was aware she was not expected to go alone. The State Department suggested that one or
two additional people might be included, but no more, and that
the persons selected should be qualified to contribute to the purposes and results of the trip.

For the next five months we were in a hyperactive state. Maurice and his team went right to work sculpturing several important new pieces for presentation to our host organizations in
China. The most impressive piece measures about 19 inches wide
by 16 inches tall by 12 inches deep. It features a pair of "Pekin
Robins" in a setting of double rhododendrons (*see color plate*).
The Pekin, like our Robin, is much loved throughout China.

The second important gift is a sculpture of a Giant Panda Cub,
one of the most delightful pieces ever issued by our studios.
Lying on its back, it is nibbling on bamboo shoots.

Over the months of August to October we were invited several
times by Mr. Chang to the Liaison Office, 2300 Connecticut
Avenue, N.W., Washington, D.C., and we became good friends.
On various occasions we met Ambassador and Mrs. Huang Chen,
Counsellor Chi Chao-chu (Harvard-educated interpreter for the
ambassador), Mr. Yang Hsu-Chiang, second secretary, and Mrs.
Wang Jung Pao, an attaché. Ambassador and Mrs. Huang

planned to visit our Trenton Studio and Mrs. Boehm's home, which they did in May 1975. One invitation we received, which we were forced to decline because of a long-standing prior commitment, was the Reception at the Liaison Office on October 1, 1974 celebrating the 25th anniversary of the founding of the People's Republic of China.

As part of our preparations for the trip I attended an excellent three-day seminar on China Trade held in New York in late August. It was an important experience as it provided an updated view of China in all respects. One of the guest speakers had considerable experience in important Chinese porcelains.

The seminar was attended by about 60 representatives of most of the top American companies, all of which are yearning for invitations to China. The potential for trade, especially in the industrial, agricultural, tele-communications, and transportation sectors, is tremendous and all want to be in a position to get a foot in the door as the climate between our countries continues to warm.

But the problems are many. An example of the difficulty in receiving an invitation by China is provided by the experience of the annual Canton Fair. Canton is located on the Pearl River Delta, 60 miles from Hong Kong. It is the sole trading port city. Only friends or people considered to be of importance to China are invited beyond Canton; and an invitation to Peking is considered very special.

About 25,000 invitations are issued for the Canton Trade Fair. It is held twice annually, April 15 to May 15 and October 25 to November 15. Each year about 50,000 Americans apply for invitations. In 1972 only 40 were received. In 1974, 250 were extended.

But U.S. trade with China is dramatically increasing. In 1971 it was only a miniscule $5 million. In 1973, as a result of the President's visit the prior year and the Shanghai Resolution of February 1972, our trade bolted to about $800 million. Over $1 billion was expected in 1974. In three years the U.S. has come from near the bottom as a trading partner to a third-rung position, surpassed now only by Japan and Hong Kong, in spite of barriers which inhibit increased trade. These barriers are:

1. Lack of full diplomatic exchange.
2. China has not been given most-favored nation status.
3. The U.S. cannot trade or bank directly with China and is forced to go through third-party countries.
4. China has no long-range credit system.
5. U.S. and China have unsettled claims against each other, $197 million vs. $71 million, respectively. (These currently are being negotiated.)
6. There is a great imbalance of trade between China and us, now 11 to 1 in our favor.

With so many odds against us, we wondered more about the reasons behind Mrs. Boehm's invitation to China. One question to which we wanted a more complete answer was why an invitation was extended to Mrs. Boehm? No doubt the deep friendships which had been established over two years had much to do with it, but there were practical reasons as well. The consensus at the seminar seemed to be:

1. China may wish to increase its exports of non-essential products to gain useful foreign exchange to purchase capital goods.
2. China's most important resource is its 800 million people. It recognizes that in time its handicrafts and arts could dominate the world market. They want to associate their porcelain with internationally-known producers. They recognize the superb quality of Boehm porcelain.
3. America is potentially their biggest market for arts and handicrafts. China may wish to learn American methods of distribution, marketing, pricing, etc. from Boehm and ascertain the receptivity of the American market to their exports, especially porcelains.
4. The Chinese are interested in promoting their products,

especially those from their light industries. They were the first to make fine porcelains and they want more people to know about it. The promotional fallout from Mrs. Boehm's trip is welcomed by them.

As for ourselves, we have a genuine desire to establish friendships with the Chinese, but a most exciting attraction for us is the prospect of visiting some of China's porcelain production centers, especially Ching-te-Chen, the fabled city hidden in a remote mountainous area toward the middle of the vast country.

Ching-te-Chen is the ancient capital of porcelain-making where artists and craftsmen started developing their fine clay formulae long before the birth of Christ, and from which beautiful art porcelains flowed centuries before the West had heard of the medium. Ching-te-Chen is the mecca of porcelainists, the ultimate standard of creativity and perfection.

Our specific wishes are to meet the outstanding artists and craftsmen, see the ancient Imperial kilns, feel the superb white clays unique to the Kaoling Hills north of the city, compare the present work with that of the past, study the techniques and qualities and share our own ways and results. What better way to gain perspective on our contemporary contributions to the art of porcelain?

The fact that no American has visited Ching-te-Chen in many years, the recognition the invitation represents, the possibility of establishing a future business relationship or an exchange program, and the chance of gaining fresh ideas and concepts are secondary but still important considerations as we plan for the trip.

The field of ceramics is complicated, its history long and confusing, and few have a good knowledge of the expressions and techniques we hope to see and describe in China. In order to assist those interested in the porcelain narratives throughout this journal (which should comprise a considerable part of it), the next three chapters are devoted to a brief summary of the technical creation and historical background of the world's fine art ceramics through the ages.

CHAPTER III

The Ceramic Media

THERE ARE REASONS for confusion and general lack of agreement in porcelain history on facts of production, origins of pieces, and styles of manufacture. Although the Chinese have been making various qualities of porcelain for close to 1,500 years, it has been less than three centuries since the arcanum was rediscovered in the West. Mysteries of the formulae which eluded early Western studios and their royal patrons greatly enhanced the attraction of the fine ceramic media, especially porcelain.

So precious were the secrets of manufacture that the first monarchs in the West had the formulae protected and their studios built under stringent secrecy measures. Studios were placed in isolated regions away from centers of population. Secrets of manufacture were imparted only to a trusted few; records were not kept and pieces often were unmarked so they could not be traced back to their origins. Fine porcelains had the equivalent value of gold, silver, and precious gems.

Adding to the confusion were the various production centers which burgeoned forth in the early to late 18th century. As new studios were built in a given production center such as Ching-te-Chen, Dresden, Staffordshire, Stoke-on-Trent and Limoges, each would claim a unique recipe, style or design, and a suitable, different trade name would have to be found. The result was the development of a trade vocabulary in each production center somewhat different from those developing simultaneously in other centers. Thousands of new small studios opened in these areas, each claiming a new quality and excitement. So for stu-

15

dents and connoisseurs of ceramics, specialization of interest is imperative.

When attempting to categorize different types of fine ceramics, therefore, one cannot deal in trade names. A separation can be made only in technical terms.

There are three basic groups of ceramics—earthenware, stoneware, and porcelain. Earthenware is a low-fired ceramic body comprised of impure clays exposed to kiln temperatures in the 1250° to 1500°F range. Without vitrification the body is porous, granular in structure. When broken, the individual grains of clay can be seen; it is much like breaking a piece of dense, hard bread or cake. It is brittle, without translucency. Colors sink into it quickly and it is heavily cast because of its relatively low strength. Some of the better-known earthenwares are delftware, redward, terracotta, faience, and majolica.

Stoneware is an earthenware-type composition fired at much higher temperatures, in the 2000°F zone. Some fusible materials, primarily feldspar, are added to the kaolins along with flint (silica) for strength and whiteness. The result is a hard, vitrified body with great strength. It differs from porcelains primarily in the fact that little or no translucent-giving materials are in the mix. Good contemporary examples of stoneware are Wedgwood's Jasperware and Basaltware.

Porcelain is a translucent form of stoneware which is fired at temperatures up to approximately 2400°F. Because of translucency, the finest and whitest kaolins must be selected, purified and carefully refined. Other additives, primarily feldspar and silica, must be similarly selected and treated. Feldspar is the flesh of high-fired ("hard") porcelain. It fuses, binds the nonfusible kaolins and silicas into a molten mass, and gives translucency. When fusing and vitrifying from a granular to a semi-molten state, porcelain shrinks an enormous 15 to 20%, creating complex technical and artistic considerations.

A variety of "soft-paste" porcelains are also made, the translucency coming from additives other than feldspar. Low-fired, vitreous bodies can be formulated by the addition of sand or rock crystal; but the composition is frivolous in the kilns because of its instability, and not receptive to properly fired colors. Alabaster, steatite and chalk can be used. The most effective "soft" porcelains are those which add a percentage of calcined ox bone. Bone withstands high kiln temperatures and has excellent plasticity; moreover, it imparts a beautiful translucency and whiteness of a quality to rival the finest of hard porcelains.

The color and texture of ceramics can take many forms and appearances. Those without the addition of glazes or enamels are called bisque (white bisque if no color is added, or decorated bisque, both of which are used extensively in our Boehm studios). The Chinese developed a white bisque called *blanc de Chine* (which also was made with a glaze finish). Artists and craftsmen of England made popular a matte-white soft-paste called parian. The bisque body is used primarily for statuary. With it one can effect a smooth, natural finish with infinite detail which is not obscured by the gloss and thickness of glaze and enamel coverings. Mr. Boehm originally adopted this finish in order to depict, with realism, the flora and fauna of our world.

Glaze is a glass-like coating which renders a body impervious to liquids and impurities in the air. High-fired, feldspathic glaze is applied to the unfired clay object (greenware) so the clays and glaze form a closely-knit body in the intense heat of the kiln. A low-fired, lead-based glaze may be used by covering a bisque piece and refiring at lower temperatures, the technique most used in the West. Enamels are low-fired glazes (glass) to which metallic oxides have been added.

Ground metallic pigments are used in coloring ceramics. When painted directly on greenware, before glazing and the first firing, the process is called under-glaze decoration. The result is a smooth, soft appearance caused by the colors sinking into the body and slightly diffusing under the glaze. The palette of colors which can stand this high fire (about 2400°F) is limited to iron, cobalt and copper oxides. Of course these colors also may be mixed into the clays or into the glaze, or both. Historically, these colors were the first to be used and perfected.

If a piece is colored after it has been glazed, the technique is called over-glaze decoration. The colors or enamels then must undergo additional firings (the number depending on the colors used) to fix the colors and sink them into the glaze. Each palette of colors can be defined by the temperatures at which they mature with the porcelain. The first family of lower-fired colors, named *famille verte*, was developed by the Chinese late in the 17th century. Copper greens of varying shades are dominant but iron reds are prevalent as well as purple, aubergine, yellow and coral. The lowest fired palette followed in the 18th century. It is called *famille rose*. Pink is the primary color along with black, lavender, blue, salmon, mauve, yellow and gold.

This brief discussion of colors is highly simplified. There are so many variables which affect the pigments—the vehicle or solution in which they are carried for application; chemical makeup and impurities; weight of color used, compatability of colors adjacent to, or on top of, others; length and level of exposure to heat; density and purity of the body on which applied; and so on. The color kiln firings are most critical. Good oxygen flow through a kiln creates an oxidizing atmosphere generally resulting in more brilliant colors. A kiln with little oxygen flow is smoky, forming concentrations of carbon dioxide which affect the colors in a different way, either changing them completely or muting the colors.

CHAPTER IV

Chinese Ceramics, Historical Highlights

THE CHINESE love pottery and porcelain. Through the centuries, beginning about 6500 B.C., they considered the sensual and aesthetic pleasure of things in a philosophical and religious way. The beautiful shape of a pot, its smooth, cool feel, aberrations and irregularities caused by human hands, its origin from the earth, the interpretation of the artist or craftsman, and the transformation of substance and color in the raging heat of the kilns. As early as the Stone Age they perfected a fine-grained, hard redware. Evidence of glazing dates back a few centuries before Christ; and feldspathic stoneware, precursor of true hard porcelain, began evolving during the Han Dynasty 206 B.C. to A.D. 220.

A review of Chinese porcelain history allows mention only of innovative changes in composition of the media, form, style and color. To place them in the long chronology covering several thousand years, it is helpful here to list the Dynasties.

HSIA	B.C.	2205–1766
SHANG	B.C.	1766–1122
CHOW	B.C.	1122–770
SPRING & AUTUMN ANNALS	B.C.	770–476
WARRING STATES	B.C.	476–221
CHIN	B.C.	221–206
HAN	B.C.	206–A.D. 220
THREE KINGDOMS	A.D.	220–265
TSIN	A.D.	265–420
SOUTHERN & NORTHERN	A.D.	420–589

SUI	A.D.	589–618
TANG	A.D.	618–907
FIVE DYNASTIES & TENKINGDOMS	A.D.	907–960
SUNG	A.D.	960–1280
YUAN	A.D.	1280–1368
MING DYNASTY	A.D.	1368–1644

Hung Wu	A.D.	1363–1399
Chien Wen	A.D.	1399–1403
Yung Lo	A.D.	1403–1425
Hung Hsi	A.D.	1425–1426
Hsuan Teh	A.D.	1426–1436
Cheng T'ung	A.D.	1436–1450
Ching Tai	A.D.	1450–1457
Tien Shun	A.D.	1457–1465
Cheng Hua	A.D.	1465–1488
Hung Chih	A.D.	1488–1506
Cheng Teh	A.D.	1506–1522
Chia Ching	A.D.	1522–1567
Lung Ching	A.D.	1567–1573
Wan Li	A.D.	1573–1620
Tai Chang	A.D.	1620–1621
Tien Chi	A.D.	1621–1628
Chung Cheng	A.D.	1628–1644

CHING DYNASTY	A.D.	1644–1911

Shun Chih	A.D.	1644–1662
Kang Hsi	A.D.	1662–1723
Yung Cheng	A.D.	1723–1736
Chien Lung	A.D.	1736–1796
Chia Ching	A.D.	1796–1821
Tao Kuang	A.D.	1821–1851
Hsien Feng	A.D.	1851–1862
Tung Chih	A.D.	1862–1875
Kuang Hsu	A.D.	1875–1908
Hsuan Tung	A.D.	1908–1911

The earliest earthenwares primarily were red, black, brown or gray caused by clays high in iron content. Clays were not mixed, nor were there additives. Gradually it was learned that the addition of sand or other kinds of supportive materials helped give the clay strength in the making and drying as well as in the kiln. Initially the vessels were formed by rolling the clay into ropes, then gradually building them up similar to a log cabin structure, smoothening and joining the clays with the hands. Often a woven basket would be used as the form to build on, later burning away from the clay in the kiln.

The earliest kilns were merely open fires fueled by wood; so the firing atmospheres were heavily oxidized. As the fires gradually closed up into cave or brick kilns, oxygen input was cut back and the reduction atmosphere caused changes in the primary iron colors.

The Shang Dynasty, 1766 B.C. to A.D. 1122, saw the development of stoneware, white pottery and high-fired glazes. With the improvement of the kilns, temperatures were raised to approximately 2000°F. This was accomplished by sealing the kilns and stoking them for about 24 hours. The effect was that of a pressure cooker. Three to five days of cooling had to be allowed before reopening the kilns. Often the entire lot was defective because of the uneven, uncontrolled heat.

Apart from feldspathic stoneware, innovations during the Han Dynasty included charcoal-fired kilns, feldspathic glazed earthenware and stoneware, and primitive colors under the glaze. One of the most beautiful colors ever achieved, certainly the most important to the Chinese through the centuries, is celadon, a palette of deep, soft greens ranging from an olive color to light blue-green. Pieces covered with feldspathic slip (liquid clay) and glazes rich in iron and fired in closed (reduction) kilns first produced the celadons sometime between the Han and Sui Dynasties. During the Sui, A.D. 589–618, the high-fired palette continued to expand by mixing iron and copper oxides; and, of great historical importance, the stoneware body had now evolved to a feldspathic porcelaneous stoneware with a clear feldspathic glaze.

The Tang Dynasty, A.D. 618–907, was a period of accelerating change in Chinese ceramics. Thinner, purer glazes and more refined bodies were mastered. The "true" porcelain body was perfected. Three-color lead glazes were used on the pottery subjects in interesting combinations, sometimes mixed together to form a marbleized finish. Some blue, yellow-orange, green and cream glazes appeared. And the period was one of great commercial activity between China and her neighbors in India, the Middle East, Persia, Japan, Korea and the southeastern islands. All were eager to visit, and to trade with, the mysterious country in the East, Cathay, the "land of silk." Merchants came by sea following the coastline from Egypt; and they came by land over the Tartary Road from Europe through the Slavic countries, north of the Caspian Sea, staying above the rugged mountains to Mongolia, and then into China. The influx of foreign ideas and images were creative stimuli to Chinese ceramics. As example, subjects most often associated with this period are the Tang horses which were inspired by Iranian and Arab horsemen and polo teams.

The period A.D. 907–A.D. 1280 covered the Five Dynasties, Tenkingdoms and the Sung Dynasty. Great progress was made in kiln construction and efficiency. Long tunnel-type kilns were built vertically against hills with steps adjacent and platforms at intervals for loading. These were over 100 feet long and accommodated upward of 10,000 pieces at a time. The firing chambers were divided into high-fired and low-fired zones. Glazes continued to become more varied and different colored slips were used over pieces, sometimes carving through one or more layers before glazing and firing, and introducing colors in various combinations. Crackled glazing was done extensively, a technique of mismatching a high-fire body with a low-fired glaze, then force-cooling. Dominant colors were celadon, black, brown, white, buff, green, and some blue. Three-color glazing continued to be refined. Decorative motifs, incised or painted, or both, expanded to include flowers (predominantly peonies), birds, animals, phoenixes and human figures.

The Mongols overran China and established the Yuan Dynasty, A.D. 1280–1368, led first by the feared Genghis Khan, then by his grandson, Kublai. Marco Polo traveled from Venice during this period, arriving in 1274 for a visit that was to last 17 years. Diversification of shapes, colors and techniques slowed a bit due to the wars and upheavals at the beginning and end of the Mongol reign. Celadons continued their ascendency because they were favorites of traders from near and far and highly prized in the palaces and courts of these lands. Although some evidence exists that blue and white underglaze porcelain was made as far back as the late Tang Dynasty, it first gained importance during the Yuan. Also developed at this time was the equally beautiful underglaze copper red. The blue was derived from cobalt oxide imported from the Middle East; the red from indigenous copper oxide. Work under the glaze included incising sgraffito (carving through a colored layer of slip to reveal an underlying slip of another color), and relief decoration, the latter by molding, modeling and appliqué.

The Chinese regained control from the Mongol Emperors late in the 14th century. This marked the beginning of the Ming Dynasty which was to span the years A.D. 1368–1644. An intellectual and cultural resurgence took place, and the arts and China prospered. Lacquer work, bronze, cloisonné, carvings— all fine arts were brought to great heights. And there were technical innovations which accelerated progress. Like Imperial tastes before them, the earlier Ming Emperors preferred subtle monochrome decoration; but polychrome wares gradually became the vogue, first in two color combinations, eventually in five (red, yellow, green, violet, blue). Blue and white attained perfection. *Blanc de Chine* was popular. New variations included whiteware with "hidden" decoration (subtle modeling and carving on whiteware), polychromes in layered relief, open and cutout cloisonné techniques, reserve decoration (leaving incised designs on pieces unglazed for later enameling), contrasting color (a beautiful technique of underglaze blue and white with overglaze enamels). Gold leaf was used for the first time. Decorative motifs expanded in all directions. Ching-te-Chen was named the Imperial production center in the late 14th century and has continued to the present to be the most important factor in fine Chinese ceramics. Chinese artists and craftsmen began to design for export, initially to the Middle East in the 15th century. Portuguese traders were the first "Westerners" to reach Canton early in the 16th century, followed later by the Dutch. Only blue and white was made for export.

The end of the Ming period began another decline for China. A struggle for power led to warring, discontent and depression. Much of China was destroyed over a span of several decades including Ching-te-Chen which was burned to the ground in 1673. Finally the Manchus took power and founded the Ching Dynasty, A.D. 1644–1911, and order and progress were restored. Under the Manchu Emperors China became the greatest power in Asia wielding influence militarily, politically, intellectually, commercially and culturally. Ching-te-Chen was rebuilt and in operation again by 1682, and the world's greatest era ever of fine ceramic production was under way. Stimulating this were the large trading companies that followed the Portuguese and Dutch. England, Germany, France, Spain, Korea, Denmark, Sweden, Russia, the United States and Japan all sent trade missions to China. None was allowed beyond the port area of Canton. All were mistrusted, but trade was allowed so long as Chinese laws and customs were adhered to strictly.

Most export porcelain was produced in Ching-te-Chen and transported south by land and river the 600 miles to Canton. Some also traveled the Yangtze to Nanking, then down the coast to the trading city. Chinese agents called "hongs" would convey the orders and designs to the Imperial production center. Soon decorating companies were built at the docks in Canton in order to expedite work and in the interest of better design execution.

The great Ching periods, which span the years A.D. 1644–1911, were during the reigns of Emperors K'ang Hsi, A.D.

1662–1723, Yung Cheng, A.D. 1723–1736 and Chien Lung, A.D. 1736–1796. Pastes, designs, textures and colors now bore the fruit of centuries of evolving artistry and craftsmanship. High-fired glazes were perfected (brown, peach bloom, celadon, blue, shiny black and *sang de boeuf* or ox blood); the *famille verte* palette appeared, followed by the low-fire *famille rose* colors. The rose colors were called "foreign" by the Chinese as they apparently were introduced by European Jesuit missionaries. An extremely wide range of porcelains was produced, spurred by the merging and crossing of Western and Chinese ideas.

The rest of Chinese history in fine ceramics has its peaks and valleys, but the experience over the last century and a half has been one of general decline. No doubt this was somewhat fostered by the gradual opening of China's ports and interior regions, influences of increasing commerce, and periodic occupation by foreign countries. But in spite of the paucity of great work from China in recent decades, and all that has been lost through centuries of pilferage and destruction, the world has been enriched by its enormous contributions to the knowledge and appreciation of fine ceramics.

CHAPTER V

Western Ceramics

IN THE LATE 13th century Marco Polo had brought back to the West with him examples of the precious high-fired ceramics of China. In fact, the first varieties he examined while in the Land of Silk must have been *blanc de Chine*. He said their beautiful whiteness and smooth texture reminded him of a sea shell, Genus *porcellana*. And so the "new" medium was named by the best known of all travelers to China.

As pieces of fine porcelain trickled west and the doors of China remained closed to most countries, monarchs of the 14th to 17th centuries began to vie with each other in attempts to assemble collections. The West had come out of the dark middle centuries and were moving toward the Renaissance. An important measure of wealth, prestige and taste came to be the size of one's Chinese export collection.

At the time the ceramic experience of the West had been in the development of earthenware and stoneware. To the collectors of the day, a comparison of these to the bright, hard, light, translucent Chinese pieces was like comparing ormolu to gold. Chemists and alchemists were set to work in attempts to duplicate the arcanum. The monarchs understood the importance of finding the formula of hard porcelain.

The search proved to be long and elusive. Many thousands of experiments were conducted from the 15th to the late 17th centuries, all without success. These were major hurdles to overcome. Knowledge of the correct ingredients was one; raising temperatures to approximately 2400°F was another.

The first soft-paste body was believed to have been made in

Florence, Italy under the patronage of Francesco de Medici about 1580. Chemists mixed glass with clays and produced a vitreous, low-fire body. The studio lasted only about ten years. Although its work pleased few, this was an important step in the direction of high-fire porcelain.

Of course, refinements in stoneware and earthenware continued to move forward and gained impetus from Chinese wares. The tin glaze earthenware pieces, first begun in the Sung, primarily were copies because they had the whiteness of hard porcelain. The clays were covered with a white slip, glazed, and painted over with enamels. Early Western examples are delftware (Holland), majolica (Italy) and faience (French).

Staffordshire potters in England continued to refine their earthenwares. Redware and terracotta were dominant in the 16th and 17th centuries. In the 18th century creamware became popular, a high-fire, fine, light-colored earthenware. Calcined flints gave whiteness and hardness to the body. And this, of course, led to the development of stoneware bodies. Early producers of these wares were Wood (c. 1750), Whieldon (c. 1754), Leeds (c. 1758), Wedgwood (c. 1759) and Spode (c. 1770).

French experiments about 1673 in Rouen resulted in a soft-paste porcelain in appearance and composition much like later English soft-pastes. Others were started at St. Cloud (c. 1673), Chantilly (c. 1725), Mennecy (c. 1734) and Vincennes (c. 1745). In 1753 the Vincennes factory was moved to Sèvres between Paris and Versailles at the request of Madame de Pompadour. With the approval of Louis XV she became active in the porcelain works. Sèvres became one of the world's most important centers, producing tablewares, in particular, that are among the most beautiful ever made. Cobalt and gold decoration were perfected and the magnificent pompadour rose color was formulated. Many believe the pompadour influenced the Chinese to develop the low-fire *famille rose* palette which, it will be recalled, they referred to as "foreign" colors.

German chemists were working primarily with stoneware

bodies. Augustus the Strong, Elector of Saxony from 1694 to 1733, was a devotee of Chinese porcelain and fully supported the search for the formula. He appointed Ehrenfried von Tschirnhausen, a nobleman and chemist, to lead the research. Von Tschirnhausen willingly accepted the challenge, as he was appalled at the huge sums of money Augustus was spending on his Chinese export collection, heavily taxing his people to do so. Saxons viewed China as the "bleeding bowl" of their country.

In 1699 an alchemist named Johann Friedrich Böttger joined von Tschirnhausen. They worked a total of fifteen years in the City of Dresden. In 1708 they combined alabaster with kaolin and silica, succeeded in creating high kiln temperatures, and made a porcelaneous stoneware. In time the alabaster was replaced by the preferred vitrifying material, feldspar. The West finally had rediscovered the arcanum, at least twelve centuries after the Chinese!

To better protect his formula Augustus moved the studio to Meissen, an isolated town about twelve miles from Dresden, and established the production in a large fortress. Meissen operated under a cloak of secrecy for two decades. The formula eventually spread as craftsmen escaped from Meissen with the aid of envious, wealthy, royal patrons; but Meissen dominated in the first half of the 18th century; and the work was superb, especially while the art direction was under the outstanding modeler, Johann Joachim Kaendler.

In 1719 and 1720 ex-Meissen craftsmen helped establish hard-paste factories in Vienna and Venice. Others followed: Hochst (c. 1746), Furstenberg (c. 1747), Nymphenburg (c. 1753), Frankenthal (c. 1755) and Ludwigsburg (c. 1758). Gradually it spread to other countries. Royal Copenhagen, famous for its hard-paste, under-glaze decoration, was started about 1772.

New English factories sprang up which modified the French-type soft-pastes: Chelsea (c. 1743), Bow (c. 1748), Derby (c. 1751), Longton Hall (c. 1751) and Lowestoft (c. 1757). The

latter has an interesting history because it is most closely inter-
woven with Chinese history, confused with it, in fact. For decades many Western collectors inaccurately referred to all
Chinese export porcelains as "Oriental Lowestoft." Lowestoft was
a village on the east coast of England which, in the 18th century,
produced a very limited supply of soft-paste porcelain. For
added business, it imported and sold foreign wares including
Delft earthenware and a lot of Chinese hard-paste. It also decorated imported white Chinese pieces and "over painted" others.
To completely complicate matters, like the Chinese export porcelains, Lowestoft didn't mark its wares.

In 1749 one of the original Bow patent holders, Thomas Frye,
was the first to introduce a quantity of bone ash into the soft-
paste formula. This was refined and later perfected by Josiah
Spode in 1794. The standard English bone body is about 25%
china clay, 25% feldspar and 50% calcined ox bone.

Worcester (c. 1751) led a small group of English studios
that were somewhat influenced by German and Chinese hard-
paste. Plymouth (c. 1768) and Bristol (c. 1770) followed. In
time, many of the above-named factories produced a variety of
hard and soft pastes; but the English always will be best known
for their bone bodies.

In the late 18th and early 19th centuries, other important English factories were begun: Caughley, Minton, Coalport, Rock-
ingham, to name a few. Royal Doulton and the present Royal
Crown Derby were started during the latter part of the 19th
century.

Through the middle of the 19th century, export porcelain
continued to come from China. The productions of East and
West gradually merged; techniques, qualities and marks were
copied back and forth and, as the West gained in experience and
output, Chinese wares went into decline. Major disruptions oc-
curred during the Opium War, 1840–1842, the combined French
and English invasion in 1860 and the Boxer Rebellion a few
years later. Ching-te-Chen again was destroyed in 1853, and

again rebuilt about 1864. Chinese productions since then have become a minor factor in Western porcelain interests.

American experience in fine ceramics has been limited and late-developing. Our trade with the Orient began with the sea voyage of the *Empress of China* which reached Canton in 1784. We've since relied heavily on porcelain exports from all over the world. Our first recorded ceramic studio was established about 1685 near Burlington, New Jersey by John Tatham, an agent of the Queen visiting the American colonies. Earthenware studios were started over the next 150 years or so, many of them in the Trenton, New Jersey area because of the relatively good clays on the eastern shore, coal from Pennsylvania for the kilns and the navigable Delaware River for transportation.

Earthenware studios in other areas also won prominence and collector followings; Burlington in Vermont and Rookwood in Cincinnati are examples. Some soft-paste studios were established in the late 19th century; and the Lenox factory of Trenton became well-known for its creamy feldspathic porcelain which was developed from Irish beleek. The only firm that had a modicum of recognition for hard-paste was Tucker, located near Philadelphia about the middle of the 19th century. It had difficulty with quality control and high losses and produced only for a period of about ten years.

Prior to Edward Marshall Boehm's venture, which began in a basement studio in Trenton in 1950, few, if any, American studios developed a high quality hard-paste porcelain combined with an excellence of design that successfully compared with the centuries-old productions of Europe and Asia. The marvel is that he accomplished this without governmental or royal subsidization, without formal art education or ceramic experience.

The foregoing review of ceramic history is brief and sketchy, but it sets the stage for our visit to China. One can readily understand our eagerness and excitement. We are about to expose our porcelain art to the grand masters; and we will be privileged to study the state of Chinese ceramics as it is today.

Fashioning a link chain cut from a solid jade block
at the Peking Fine Arts and Handicrafts Factory.

CHAPTER VI

Peking

BACK TO OUR FLIGHT somewhere between Karachi and Peking. A luncheon is served which maintains Air France's standard of excellence. Finally we are told we soon will be making our descent into the Peking area. We are given a long and detailed customs form to fill out. Among the three of us we have a difficult time. We had to list and define each piece of jewelry by maker, style and value; all foreign currency with us; number of rolls of film, movie cameras and transistors; valuable clothing; etc. Our French stewardesses come to the rescue.

It is difficult to see much during our descent. A misty grayness hangs like a veil over everything. Gradually we can define neatly squared off agricultural plots, an interlacing network of irrigation troughs and small clusters of brick and adobe-type homes forming individual communes. As we come in for our landing at Peking Airport, dozens of Chinese pause for a moment from their agricultural duties to watch our plane pass. Some wave.

We step from the plane and are impressed immediately by a massive color photograph of Chairman Mao in the center facade of the airport terminal, flanked by his statements in huge red characters. The photograph must measure about six yards square. We would see images of the Chairman often on most official and semi-official buildings throughout the country; and whereas American billboards carry advertisements of products, China's billboards carry the teachings of Mao.

Our passage through customs is interesting. We later learned the officials were told to allow us through quickly with no delay, but no one told them how to recognize us. Mrs. Boehm had no problems, as usual. I had a few. It was Maurice Eyeington who faced a dilemma. Under "occupation" on his customs forms he had written "sculptor." They wanted to know what that meant. Maurice called us over and asked if we would help explain "what I am," upon which we were rescued by our hosts who came in to investigate our delay.

We are met by Mr. Hu Hung-fan, and Mrs. Chang Hsueh-ling, of the Chinese People's Association for Friendship with Foreign Countries. Mr. Hu is one of the chief counsellors. Mrs. Chang is a colleague who has been assigned to accompany us during our entire stay in China. Both speak English well. Their ages seem to be in the early to mid-40s. Also with them is a Mr. Chou Hsin-pei, a delightful young man. He has had five years of English at Shanghai University. Like Mrs. Chang, Mr. Chou will travel with us throughout China.

Two cars are awaiting us, both called "Shanghai," made in the city of the same name. They remind us of the late 1940s Packards, roomy and comfortable. Our luggage disappears and magically finds its way to our hotel.

The drive from the airport consumes about forty minutes. Of course we are keenly aware of everything as we approach the city. The road we're on is absolutely straight, obviously rebuilt recently, and higher than the adjacent lands. Deep parallel ditches on each side of the road form sloughs, beyond which are fields of winter wheat, fruit trees and, to our surprise, vineyards. Protective trees, carefully placed like soldiers, line the highway.

We quickly are made aware of the more than 2 million bicycles in Peking and the constantly blaring bells and horns. The cyclists seem to ignore the automobiles and there is a continuing contest for road space. Thousands are coming and going and there is no dilly-dallying. It is something like well-organized confusion.

The manner of dress has great impact. There are two basic uniforms, military green and civilian blue. Men and women wear the same clothing. No dresses are seen. It is difficult for us to

A hand-carved wood screen in Foshan. Notice the similar dress worn by men and women.

separate sexes because of short hair and caps. Occasionally a pair of long braids will appear to define a female.

The sameness of the dress creates a uniformity of color everywhere, which is not alleviated by the fine cloud of dust that hangs in the air. Peking is very dry this time of year and the gray-brown silt that is kicked up, along with the coal-burning soot, coats everything, the streets, buildings and trees. Those with respiratory problems wear white surgical masks as they travel the city. The huge red teachings of Mao printed along the streets on walls and buildings seem to be the only color relief.

A most important first impression is the friendliness of all of the people. Smiles greet us constantly and there is always someone waiting to open a door, carry a package, lend a service in some way. One immediately feels welcome and comfortable. It is easy to feel warmth for these gracious people.

We are fortunate to be staying at the Peking Hotel on "Boulevard of Peace," a tremendous, straight road which measures 50 meters in width and is 30 kilometers long. There are three connecting wings to the hotel. The first, still bearing the designs and decor of the past, is over 100 years old. In the center is a wing which was built about fifteen years ago. It forms a transitional bridge in style and decor between the old and new wings, the latter having been completed just recently. Together the wings total about 900 rooms. We learned later that an average room with meals is about $6 (12 yuan in renmimbi) a day; a suite can go as high as $50.

We are in the new wing. It is modern and impressive. The main lobby is bigger than those of most hotels we've seen. Elevators are automatic, although operators are present. Keys hang on a desk board and are gathered as we debark from the elevator. I suppose the keys are primarily to make visitors content. There is no real need for them as there is no theft in China. We would take frivolous delight in leaving our doors unlocked at all times all over China.

Mr. Hu and Mrs. Chang stay with us until about 5:30, telling us, over excellent tea, the itinerary they have planned. It is spectacular beyond our dreams and includes a two-day visit to Ching-te-Chen! We are told we can take photographs inside the studios with the artists and craftsmen and any notes we desire. Our hosts make it clear they wish us to thoroughly discuss and trade ideas and techniques. We look forward to doing so.

Our itinerary:

Nov. 30—Visit the "Peking Fine Arts and Handicrafts Factory." Luncheon with the Vice Chairman Li of the Association for Friendship, and presentation of our gifts. In the evening we'll take a three-hour train ride to Tangshan.

Dec.   1—Tour Tangshan's porcelain factories.

Dec.   2—Return to Peking on noon train. Stay for 3rd and 4th. We'll see other art factories and also spend an evening with Ambassador and Mrs. George Bush at the U.S. Embassy.

Dec. 5—Fly to Hangchow to see arts and handicrafts factories.

Dec. 7—Fly to Nanchang; then take a car and drive to Ching-te-Chen. Visit three porcelain factories.

Dec. 10—Back to Nanchang; then fly to Shanghai to see more fine arts factories.

Dec. 13—Fly from Shanghai to Kuangchou (Canton).

Dec. 14—Tour Foshan's stoneware and earthenware factories.

Dec. 15—Leave Canton for Hong Kong.

Our hosts leave and we relax with a drink and exchange feelings and anticipations about our great adventure. We also assess our rooms and the services and quickly find that we've brought too much of everything with us. The rooms are attractive with modern baths, hot and cold water, soft tissue, adequate lighting, excellent firm beds, telephone, bedside light and room service controls, a lot of space and bureaus for clothes, good towels and soap, and the ever-present tea. Hot water for tea always is available in large thermos jugs that hold about two quarts of water.

The hotel has a special dining room for foreign visitors capable of seating 100 or more. There are about forty for dinner, Germans, Chinese, Africans, Southeast Asians and quite a number of Japanese among them.

We are assigned a table and an English-speaking waiter. Dinner consists of an outstanding beef soup, sauteed eggs and mushroom stems, rice and sweet and sour swordfish fillets. We quickly discover that although the orange pop is not to our taste, the beer is excellent.

After dinner we willingly head for bed and collapse in exhaustion. Maurice and I are assigned to one large room. Mrs. Boehm's room is adjacent.

We breakfast at 7:30 this morning, November 30. Our waiter suggests eggs and bacon. We each have three well-prepared eggs sunny-side up and excellent toast and jam. At 8:10 we're on our way to visit the Peking Fine Arts and Handicrafts Company. Again (as was to be the case throughout our entire trip) we are provided with two cars and drivers for the five of us.

Driving through Peking is fascinating. It is a city of contrasts; gleaming, recently-erected buildings and old temples; oxen and donkeys; every conceivable type of vehicle from the most ancient cart to the modern auto.

The minute division of labor immediately manifests itself. The Chinese have no unemployment. All are busy and responsible. And the city, like all of China, is immaculate and neat. People are constantly sweeping the streets and picking up debris. Cleanliness is combined with thrift. Cow and horse dung collectors roam the streets and what is gathered eventually winds up back on the farms.

The Peking Fine Arts and Handicrafts Company is a series of large square buildings broken into small studio rooms. About 1300 artists and craftsmen are employed. This is the biggest in the country. Branches, all of which come under the aegis of the Light Industries Corporation, are located in many of the major cities.

The revolutionary council leader of the Peking company is Mr. Peng Shao-chi, a small, friendly man whose official title is Vice-Chairman. We sit in an attractive showroom surrounded by the magnificent artistry of his associates and enjoy the first of many cups of tea and good Chinese cigarettes in a red pack labeled "Chungwa, Shanghai Cigarette Factory, China." The Chinese whom we will see smoke more than the average American.

An impressive list of arts and crafts are produced in this mini-conglomerate:

1. Lacquerware pieces of furniture inlaid with gold, silver, jade and mother of pearl.
2. Sculptured lacquer vases, bowls and urns of a type which is known in the West as "Cinnebar." A tedious process

which requires the buildup of 100 to 300 baked coats of lacquer to obtain a thickness of about ¼". This then is carved to produce an intaglio design. The dominant color is a rusty red.

3. Ivory and jade carving. We saw dozens of carvers, young and old, working on Burmese and Chinese jade. One elderly carver was at the end of his second year on a Ming-type covered jar with a long link chain. He said 3½ years are needed to complete the piece. At most a person will do 15 in a lifetime.

4. Dough figures. These are delightful miniature figures, two or three inches in size, modeled from a dough made of a mixture of rice, wheat and honey. Little children, in the main, with cute expressions and colorful ensembles.

A delicate painting on pure Chinese silk from the Peking Fine Arts and Handicrafts Factory.

5. Cloisonné is one of the largest departments. Starting with a plain brass vase or urn, the artists draw their designs on the object, glue tiny pieces of flat brass wire on edge to conform with the drawn design resulting in relief channels about $\frac{1}{8}''$ deep, and fill the channels by hand with different colored enamels. When dry, the pieces are baked in kilns. Enameling and firing are repeated several times depending on the number of color enamels and the complexity of the designs.

6. Paintings on silk, as only the Chinese can do it.

7. Filigree work with silver. The process begins, as in cloisonné, with a silver urn or vase. The artist builds a filigree design by soldering fine strands of silver onto the form. Much heat is used to meld the whole together, followed by extensive burnishing.

8. Jewelry of all kinds, much both of jade and of enamel.

9. Interior bottle painting. This is particularly fascinating and demanding. The artists work with clear miniatures the sizes and shapes of snuff bottles. With extremely fine brushes, difficult for the eye to see, bent into 90° angles, the artist paints a scene or figure in reverse on the inside of the bottle!

The Peking company was started as recently as 1960. Studio rooms average in size 15′ x 30′ and house about 20 artists and craftsmen. Young people begin training at 14 and serve a three-year apprenticeship. Each room has a revolutionary squad leader, usually a model worker who serves as an example to the other craftsmen, and a large active bulletin board which bears Mao's teachings, work goals for the group, and spontaneous individual expressions concerning efforts and production. We are told that the company is very productive, "although it strives to do even better," and that exports go to about ninety different countries.

Mr. Peng is a gentle and gracious man who came up through the ranks as a cloisonné artist. He spoke glowingly about the

Artisans work first with clay models before carving in jade, which comes from China and Burma.

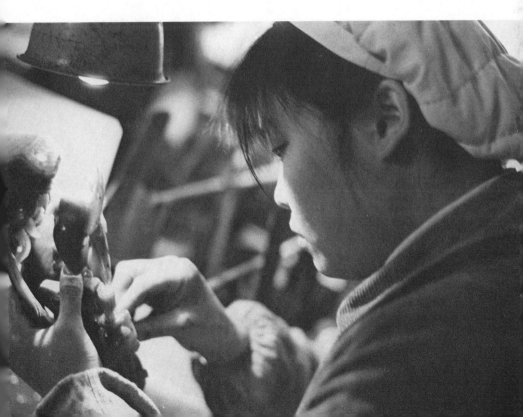

arts and his company and always spoke of attaining even greater achievements.

The afternoon of the 30th was to provide a special treat. We warmly bade Mr. Peng and his associates our goodbyes and thanks for a fascinating morning and rushed back to the Peking Duck Restaurant for a special luncheon in our honor given by our host organization. Present were Ambassador Li En-chiu, Vice Chairman of the Chinese People's Association for Friendship with Foreign Countries, Mr. Hu, Mr. Chang, Mr. Chou and a special and honored surprise, Mrs. Huang, wife of Ambassador Huang Chen of the Washington Liaison Office. A charming, happy friend who is here with her husband for a series of meetings.

Mr. Li is charismatic. He is reserved in character, makeup and dress, wears a long, thin beard, has a constant smile and presides over the luncheon with the gracious manner of a wise elder Chinese. We later learn that Mr. Li formerly was Ambassador to the Netherlands.

Ambassador Li receives the Pekin Robins sculpture on behalf of the People's Association for Friendship with Foreign Countries. Mrs. Huang Chen, wife of the ambassador who serves as the top official in the United States, was also present.

We exchange pleasantries for about ten minutes with tea and cigarettes, then sit down to a round table for eight. Drinks first are served—mao tai, a very strong sorghum liquor of 130 proof, rice wine and beer. Mr. Li welcomes us with a short speech ended by a mao tai toast. His comments are reminiscent of those of former President Nixon and Chou En-Lai. He speaks of the long period of problems between our countries, but also of the warmth our peoples have always had for each other. "But since 1972," said he, "we've built new bridges between us which will serve to bring us closer together." And he refers to the contributions the artists of the world are making in stimulating better understanding among all peoples. He points specifically to our work and states that we are the first Americans in our field ever to be the guests of China!

Mrs. Boehm replies in brief and in kind; then we begin a luncheon that has to rank among the best that one could experience. We've always enjoyed duck, but our admiration for this winged creature increased tremendously. We are told that every part of the duck is used in some way. We think we had everything but the feathers, an eight course luncheon all of duck— foot bones, foot webs, livers, hearts, tongues and everything in between and around. At the last we have duck soup (the second serving of soup) made from duck bones. Mr. Li explains that the restaurant has specialized in duck for over 100 years; and that the Russians enjoyed it so in the 1950s that China sent five of their best chefs to Moscow about 1955 to establish a similar restaurant there although, eventually, the chefs returned to China, says Mr. Li with a smile.

At the end of the luncheon we exchange gifts. Mrs. Boehm presents the important Pekin Robins sculpture to Mr. Li for the Association and a collector's copy of our book *Edward Marshall Boehm, 1913–1969*. She receives a magnificent pair of cloisonné vases; Maurice and I are the recipients of pairs of large black lacquer vases with applied gold designs.

After lunch we have a few extra hours so Mrs. Chang and Mr. Chou take us to the "Friendship Store," a large organization on the order of a good-sized department store. The Peking shop has four floors of exquisite merchandise, clothes, furniture, home accessories, and art of all kinds. One could spend days here. The main problem is selection. In jade alone there are literally hundreds of offerings. We purchase as much as we have time for and are told we would have other opportunities to return. The Chinese allocate a generous amount of time to visitors for shopping as an added courtesy. We are told to spend as many dollars as we wish. Dollars and American Express checks are exchanged for yuan in the store.

We return to the Peking Hotel in time for dinner which we skip in view of the long and filling lunch. We are advised to pack a small bag for two nights (leaving the remainder of our luggage in our rooms), are collected at 7:30 p.m. and driven to the train station. The Peking Station is very like Penn Central or Grand Central, thousands of people milling around, running or standing in line. All seem to know we are coming. They don't, of course. Chinese courtesy dictates that guests are first. The waves of people open continuously leaving an unimpeded corridor to our train.

The three of us are given a private compartment with beds so we might rest during the three and one-half hour journey to Tangshan. The room is clean and neat. White needlepoint lace covers the seat backs. A gaily covered table with a little vase of flowers is against the windows. And, of course, there is tea. The bathroom, serving both sexes, is clean and somewhat unique. An open metal trough at floor level is straddled by two flat metal footrests. At one end of the trough is a metal hood about a foot high for which I must figure out a use.

Trains in China are unusually smooth. Mr. Chou explains that the rail sections are very long and have a tongue-and-groove joint that eliminates the rythmic bumping. He also mentions with pride that the trains are always on time.

CHAPTER VII

Tangshan's Porcelain Factories

AT 11:15 P.M. of the 30th we arrive at Tangshan Station. Just prior to debarking Mrs. Chang explains that accommodations will not be quite so good as in Peking. She isn't apologizing, just preparing us for the more modest conditions of smaller cities and villages. In her charming fashion she says, "You must remember that China is still a developing country."

We are met by Mr. How Sun-mei, Counsellor in Tangshan for the Association. The drive to the Tangshan Guest Hotel is about ten minutes, and we are in bed by midnight.

At 7:30, December 1, we have breakfast consisting of fried eggs "over lightly," toast, small fried pancakes and coffee. We notice now that Mrs. Chang and Mr. Chou do not join us for meals. It is their way of allowing us privacy and time for discussion; and, unless there is a special luncheon or dinner, two dining rooms are used, one for Chinese and one for their guests.

By 8:10 we are on our way, joined by Mr. How and his assistant. We first are taken to the central offices of the Tangshan Porcelain Company where we are met by General Shih, Revolutionary Council leader of all of the porcelain factories in Tangshan. We sit in a large room with comfortable chairs. Mr. Shih is accompanied by his general supervisor, two porcelain technicians, one designer and two secretaries. We have tea and cigarettes while General Shih officially welcomes us and tells us all about Tangshan's porcelains.

Tangshan, located in Ha Pei Province, is a relatively "new" porcelain production area dating back only about 550 years, very young compared to Ching-te-Chen! Its first studio was established

1404 during the Ming Dynasty, although pottery has been produced in the city for more than 2,000 years. The emphasis in the porcelain companies here is on household tablewares both for the home market and for export. Although the needs of the Chinese people far exceed supply, the factories of Tangshan must export 40% of their production to help increase exports.

There are fifteen porcelain factories in Tangshan which employ 11,500 artists and craftsmen. In 1974 they will produce 120,000,000 pieces of porcelain. This startles us and we gently interrupt to corroborate the figures. There is no mistake. We are to learn throughout the day that this is no exaggeration. Mr. Shih explains that every separate piece is counted as one. A saucer and cup, for example, comprise two pieces.

General Shih, whose appearance belies his age, has a military bearing the roots of which go back to the Long March with Mao. He speaks with reverence and pride about the Chairman and stresses that the success of the porcelain workers is due to their careful cognizance and adherence to Mao's dictums.

He states he has been with the porcelain companies 23 years and that the artists and craftsmen have taught him much, but that he still has much to learn. When he assumed charge of the Tangshan production area in 1958 it was comprised of twenty-three factories producing 16,000,000 pieces of porcelain. These were consolidated into fifteen; design, administrative and other functions were centralized; Mao's teachings were reemphasized and by 1965 production rose to 63,000,000. This year that will be doubled.

General Shih tells us there are some differences in remuneration among the workers. Designers and administrators are paid slightly more than others, although an outstanding production worker can earn as much. There are eight pay grades, the average being about 60 yuan ($30) a month; but we are told little money is necessary because services are free and housing, food and clothing are so inexpensive. Also, as explained by the General, costs do not fluctuate. There is no inflation.

General Shih talks about how the "workers are mobilized." The supervisors listen to the workers and make sure there is complete cooperation. "Some of the biggest advances in production and new equipment," he says, "have been developed by the workers themselves." He later emphasized this point by showing us a unique automatic mold-filling machine and introducing us to the proud craftsman who devised it.

"We stress self-reliance according to Chairman Mao," continues General Shih, "and since the liberation we have a new dedication. We do not want to rely on others, but we do want to share our products and techniques with friends."

General Shih then asks us for a brief description of our studios stating that later in the day, after we've seen some of the Tangshan production, we will have a longer meeting and exchange ideas. During our fifteen-minute dissertation Mrs. Boehm presents General Shih and Mr. How with a copy of our book, a large thirteen-inch commemorative plate with acid-etch gold border featuring images of the Mute Swan "Bird of Peace," and a copy of our 1974 color booklet.

Our first visit is to the exhibition rooms where a chronological display is simply but attractively arranged. One cabinet of pottery is dated before Christ. Another shows some of the early stonewares and porcelains made during the 15th century in Tangshan.

As we continue we soon are impressed by the versatility of the companies. Although the emphasis here is on tablewares, examples of sculpture, monumental poured-mold vases as tall as six feet, delicate flower and insect work similar to ours, painted porcelain plaques measuring one by three feet, and skillfully painted art plates all speak eloquently of the talent and versatility of the Tangshan artists and craftsmen.

General Shih, Mr. Chau, the company director, and an entourage of about two dozen administrators, designers and technicians take us on a tour of one of the large factories. As we are walking we are told by General Shih that Sunday is usually not a working day but that the entire staff gave up their day so as to be present

General Shih and Mr. How show Mrs. Boehm through the exhibition room of the Tangshan Porcelain Factory. *Below*, a view of one of the large and busy packing departments of the company.

for our visit. How can one express gratitude for such a splendid and generous gesture?

As we enter the first department, processing of the raw materials, all the workers rise as one and applaud us, a warm and friendly welcome. This is repeated everywhere we go. In some areas General Shih or Mr. Chau will introduce us to a model worker and proceed to extol his or her accomplishments so all may hear. The co-workers seem to be genuinely pleased for those receiving praise. Inherent in their system is criticism of oneself and praise, when earned, for others. The workers have an active role in appraising the efforts and results of their colleagues, and on the basis of continuous meetings and discussions, help each other set their own wage levels, production goals and behavior patterns.

The raw materials room is identical to ours. Composition of the porcelain is hard paste, with the same ingredients used in our Trenton studio's flint, various kaolins, feldspar and ball clay. Not enough care seems to be given to maintaining the cleanliness of the materials. They are stored on the concrete floor in wooden stalls and are unprotected from dirt and other foreign matter. This oversight is apparent to us in some of their finished products. The paste often shows slight discolorations and imperfections. A round tabletop we see in the exhibition rooms, featuring a magnificent tiger painting in blue underglaze, has an abundance of large imperfections caused by extraneous grit. One of the supervisors explains, "It is difficult to keep dirt particles from flying about in the heat of the kilns." We continue to see that the purity of the porcelain body in Tangshan does not quite compare with the finest work of the West.

We begin to get an idea of the tremendous volume of production. Ten huge ball mills, each of which mix about ten tons of clay, stand in a long line. Eight are in operation humming their repetitive songs caused by the shifting of quartz pebbles in the rotating metal drums. A mill half the size of one of these large ones provides more than enough slip for our entire Trenton studio needs.

We next go through the jiggering departments where dozens of men and women make the raw form of the various tableware shapes. In use here are semiautomatic jiggers. The worker takes a measured amount of clay, slaps it into a mold, spins the mold automatically, then brings down onto the clay a lever, the end of which is formed to shape the spinning clay into a plate or bowl. At the same time the excess clay is thrown off. In most of the china companies of the West this process is entirely mechanized.

Occasionally on our tour we are introduced to a small group out of the production flow which is working on a new machine. Such initiatives are encouraged in the factories. Several of the major pieces of equipment shown us developed from ideas given by workers.

The clay finishing and glazing rooms are similar in techniques and flow to our Western companies although, again, a firm like the Lenox China Company is much more heavily mechanized. We are taken through the inspection and transfer printing departments (application of decalcomanias for decoration) and finally to the handpainting division. This is what most fascinates us. Young and old sit together. Unlike the occasional selfishness of elder porcelain artists in the West who often are reluctant to share their hard-earned techniques, cooperation here seems total. No one need be concerned about being replaced or losing position.

As in the West, artists tend to specialize on subject matter they most enjoy and do best. One artist does only tigers, another only cats, another only landscapes, etc. We see none of the "bench painting" practiced during the latter half of the Ching Dynasty, where individual craftsmen would paint only part of each subject, then pass it down the line, an ancient assembly-line technique.

It is difficult to compare the quality of painting with ours. The techniques, brush strokes and designs are so different. The simplicity of their results misleads one to feel they may not be as demanding as what can be done in the West, or may not have quite the finesse of good French or English painting; but as we know from the experience of having outstanding Chinese painters on our Trenton staff, the conversion to Western techniques and subject matter can easily be made. It is a question of differences of style rather than quality of painting. The Chinese traditionally have preferred a placid, subtle, uncluttered look, simple forms using design to complement rather than adorn.

The factory we have just toured was built largely in 1958, and expansion is continuing. General working conditions are good, in fact superior to some of the factories we've seen in England. Space is excellent and all working areas are clean. The only deficiencies are the lighting and lack of heat. There is not a lot of daylight due to the absence of large windows and skylighting. Most artists and craftsmen each have a small bulb to work under. The lack of heat is most amazing. Apparently all gradually ac-

Visiting with the chief designer in the sculpturing and clay artistry division.

climate from the summer to the winter and can sit and paint fine detail in damp 40°F weather.

The work week is six days, eight hours a day. There is generally a two-hour lunch break during which the workers engage in exercise, meetings and political sessions. In the large cities factory hours are staggered in order to help ease bicycle traffic congestion!

Through the morning we are encouraged to take as many pictures as we wish, closeups of artists and group photos which include General Shih and Mr. Chau. Like people everywhere, they immensely enjoy having their pictures taken. We are allowed to speak directly to the workers and ask them any questions we wish. We have good conversation and lots of fun. And all seem to respond to the warmth of Helen Boehm as she shakes their hands and often places her arm around their shoulders in spontaneous gestures of friendship.

We leave the Tangshan factory and start back to the hotel for lunch. On the way we have time to concentrate more on this city of about half a million people located 140 miles northeast of Peking. Tangshan is an industrial city; its main productions are coal, steel, mining, machinery and ceramics. There is a pollution problem. Its rivers steam and boil. Smog and dust are so heavy the sky has a lurid, yellow-orange color. A good percentage of the populace wear their white surgical masks at all times. Energy is produced by coal, and mining is carried on in shafts dropped right in the middle of the city. Everywhere there is building activity. An endless procession of horse and mule-drawn carts moves toward the city with stones, bricks and other building materials.

The homes in Tangshan, as in Peking, are generally built behind eight- to ten-foot high stone or brick walls that close off viewing from the streets. Behind the walls are courtyards and small connecting apartments facing each other. It is virtually impossible to see any of the living activity within, only quick glimpses through open gates.

At the ceramic design and training institute in Tangshan were remarkable examples of fine clay work, including a bonsai-like tree with several thousand lifelike needles.

Our lunch at the hotel consists of egg-drop soup, tasty sword-fish fillets, cooked in a sweet and sour sauce, rice and a cooked-cauliflower salad. We are given an extra hour to rest, then are off again to visit the ceramic research, design and training institute. Here are graduated 200 students a year for the Tangshan Porcelain Company. Here also are valuable projects investigating new pastes, colors, subject matter and techniques of production.

The institute is a revelation. It is apparent that the most talented artists and craftsmen are here. The work being done is of superb quality and skill, especially in the clay area. We are introduced to the head clay designer, a lady of about thirty years of age. She shows us remarkable clay work that compares in delicacy and detail to anything we do. One piece is a large coupe-shaped thirteen inch plate on which are mounted delicate hand-made chrysanthemums and a praying mantis, thin to life, which defies description. Another is a small pine tree similar to a Japanese bonsai which must have several thousand fine lifelike needles in its construction. This is what we really have come to see. We thoroughly enjoy conversing with these talented people and we take loads of photographs.

Our hosts invite Maurice Eyeington to sculpture with their clay.

One of the sculptors generously invites Maurice to sit down and get his hands into the clay. What a remarkable experience. Here in Tangshan in a remote area of China thousands of miles from Trenton, a couple of dozen Chinese artists cluster around and excitedly watch an American artist model a clay bird. The whole meaning of our trip is summed up in this one episode.

It is about 3:30 p.m. now. We are led into a large conference room. Altogether we number about thirty people, a mixture of artists, technicians and administrators. The conversation is much more relaxed and free-wheeling this afternoon with greater participation. The handsome, ramrod-like General Shih, in his close-cut hair and trim black suit (similar to the "Nehru" look), is friendly and smiling. A lot of information is freely exchanged.

Of particular interest to our hosts is the gold acid-etch technique used on the border of the large commemorative plate presented by Mrs. Boehm. This is a process which, briefly, involves the transfer of a design to a plate using a wax stencil bearing the design, the sealed parts of which protect the plate glaze from being etched, the open parts allowing the acid through to etch according to the design. Eventually the etched areas are hand-filled with gold. The Tangshan artists have an etching technique but it is different than that developed and perfected in England. We tell them all we can and promise to send detailed information about the process.

It is a mystery to us why they are not familiar with the English techniques. The process is available to all. Perhaps we'll see it in Ching-te-Chen. We ask General Shih in what markets are sold the fine arts pieces we saw produced in the institute. He explains that these are primarily experimental and exhibition pieces which are not for sale. Making them serves many purposes including those of artistry and craftsmanship; allowing a certain amount of innovative expression; studying the limitations of the medium; testing of new clays and other materials; and the honing of teaching techniques.

General Shih's emphasis is largely on production. He states that "the artist in porcelain must be practical as well as creative and should not produce pieces that are easily broken and un-shippable." But, we say, the truly great work is worth taking risks for. What we've seen the world would yearn to share. We cannot shake him from his point. He again alludes to the huge need that still exists among the Chinese people for household tablewares and that this is where their total efforts and attentions must be focused.

General Shih goes on to talk about what he thinks the artist's philosophy should be. Fortunately, because of pauses in waiting for the translations and as a result of some army schooling in shorthand, I am able to report his remarks quite accurately. "The artist," he says, "like everyone else, has a responsibility to the people. He must communicate to the people through what he creates and he must attempt to communicate to as many as he can. This determines his degree of success or failure. Therefore the artist must deal with reality. He must not stray into subject areas to provide self-gratification. He must call attention to the natural beauty of our surroundings and educate the people to its harmony and values."

It is interesting to compare this statement with Chairman Mao's official pronouncement on the state of the arts in the People's Republic of China and its political, as well as artistic, function. At the Yenan Forum on Literature and Art in 1956, the Chairman said, "In the world today all culture, all literature and art, belong to definite classes and are geared to definite political lines. There is in fact no such thing as art for art's sake, art that stands above classes, art that is detached from or independent of politics. Proletarian literature and art are part of the whole revolutionary cause; they are, as Lenin said, cogs and wheels in the whole revolutionary machine."

Eventually small conversations erupt and our two interpreters are kept very busy. We particularly enjoyed talking with the head supervisor about mutual technical problems, especially about the thickness of porcelain paintings. This is the most challenging area of work because of the difficulty in firing a thin square or rectangle and the demands placed on the artist's skills. Most porcelains start with a spherical base in order to reduce warping and curling during the initial bisque firing which results in a shrinkage factor of 15% to 20%. Because of its equal radii, a sphere physically is self-compensating whether expanding or reducing, like a balloon which is gaining or losing air. The radii of a square or rectangle increase to the corners. In the process of firing, the corners have to shrink further, causing warping and curling. The loss factor in the first firing at Tangshan is eight out of ten, 80%. This is about the same as our experience. And there are occasional added losses in the subsequent decorating fires due to cracking of the thin canvases. Theirs vary from $\frac{3}{8}$ inch to 1 inch thick, ours about $\frac{1}{4}$ inch. Because of the simplicity of their colors and design, their paintings go through an average of four firings, ours an average of eight. It is comforting to learn that the vagaries and limitations of the high-fired porcelain body allow no additional respect to a company 550 years old!

After more than an hour's exchange and a lot more tea and cigarettes, we are ready to leave. General Shih thanks us for our visit and expresses the hope that we might come another time for a longer stay. Mrs. Boehm returns sincere compliments and thanks and says she looks forward to a day when perhaps we might exchange artists. This draws a response of approval from all in the room. We have a warm, rewarding feeling. We have established a genuine respect and friendship with these fine people.

On our return to the Guest Hotel we put our thoughts together in evaluating what we have seen in Tangshan. There is no question of their deep talent and experience, but it is doubtful that their efforts will be applied to our kind of art expressions because of their emphasis on mass production, increased production and the current highly pragmatic approach of the decision-makers.

Care and refinement of raw materials is good although imperfections in the paste and in the glazing are not infrequent.

Subject matter reveals some emphasis on traditional subjects, but a good percentage of the shapes, figures and painted designs stress political messages.

Painting skills are high although the styles, techniques and designs are simpler than in the West, giving one the impression they are perhaps not quite as demanding on the artists.

Research, development and training are good. In five to ten years the tableware industry here could be as highly mechanized as in the West.

Individual motivation and effort are high, as one would expect, but not for achieving personal rewards. It is stressed that competition exists, but only for the purpose of helping one to excel and to realize one's potential. General Shih expressed it as, "achieving new goals up the ladder of self-improvement and thereby contributing to socialism."

Working conditions are very good, better than in the average Western porcelain companies. The only deficiencies are in the lighting and heating.

Finally, there is no question that the Chinese of Tangshan have a respect and feeling for the medium developed through five and one-half centuries of creativity and experience. During the day we felt the sense of pride in the artists and craftsmen, many of whom have more generations than they can count in their ancient and honored art. What they strive for in fine porcelain was re-iterated by our hostess, Mrs. Chang. "Fine porcelain," she said, "must be thin as paper, white as jade, bright like a mirror, sound like a bell."

After a light dinner we are paid a visit by our official host, Mr. How, and his associate. They bring gifts for all, three beautiful, hand-painted miniature vases done by two of the artists we had met. In addition, Mrs. Boehm is given a decorative plate made in one of the studios we did not visit. This particular studio, we are told, specialized in paintings done entirely with the use of fine spray guns. The plate is remarkable. It is a scene of the lake and mountains of Hangchow, "the most beautiful city in China," which we will visit for two days next week. The artist entitled the plate "West Lake Autumn Scenery." Boats on the lake bear fig-ures of such small scale that one barely can see the fine detail of the faces. It is difficult to imagine that this was done aerographi-cally.

Frank Cosentino, Maurice Eyeington and Mrs. Helen Boehm with their guide and interpreter, Mrs. Chang, at the Great Wall.

Below: The Boehm porcelain "Bird of Peace" Mute Swans presented to Chairman Mao Tse-Tung and his people in 1972 by President Richard Nixon.

Exchanging gifts with Mr. Wong Ching-fu, Director of the Imperial Palaces, who holds the Boehm "Bird of Peace" plate. *Below*, the Boehm porcelain "Pekin Robins" presented to the Chinese People's Association for Friendship with Foreign Countries.

This magnificent eggshell porcelain bowl was purchased in Ching-te-Chen by Mrs. Boehm.

Below, life-size stone sculptures of elephants, lions, camels, tigers and dogs line the "sacred path" to the Great Ming Tombs outside Peking.

Massive bronze sculptures surround the Imperial Palaces.
The Boehm porcelain Red-billed Blue Magpie, *below*, inspired
during the tour of the Imperial Palace gardens.

CHAPTER VIII

Back to Peking

THE NEXT DAY, December 2, largely will be consumed by traveling back to Peking. The Tangshan train station is similar in size and structure to the average American station in a medium-sized city. Three sets of tracks in each direction flank the station building in the center. Access is by a pedestrian overpass. We have about fifteen minutes to wait. It is windy and bitterly cold.

While waiting we experience an unusual example of Chinese honesty and friendship. I intentionally had left an almost-wasted piece of soap and its modest plastic case at the Guest Hotel and also had thrown in a waste basket the bubblewrap packing material which had protected the plate Mrs. Boehm presented to General Shih. A few minutes before our train arrived a young man came speeding up on a bicycle. He had ridden five miles to return our property to us.

We board our train at 10:45 a.m. and will arrive at 3:00 p.m. Again our train accommodations are clean and fresh. It is a treat to see so much of China's attractive countryside. It is as one might expect, neatly-spaced and outlined farming tracts heavily irrigated, all tied together by widely-spread communes. There are not many trees in this part of China, although new ones line the train route. Mrs. Chang explains that many trees have been planted "since the liberation," especially in and around Peking. In addition to beautifying, they are important in helping shield against the brutal winter winds.

The incredible kindness and hospitality continue and seem to increase daily. Our hosts have arranged to have the dining car opened just for us! Never mind that we have to dine in an unheated car in a temperature just above freezing. We wrap blankets around us and enjoy one of the best meals so far, eight different dishes of chicken and vegetables, pork and vegetables, fried shrimp, leeks and duck, a black, leafy fungus that is superb, battered and fried swordfish, a processed ham similar to our spam, egg-drop soup, rice, beer and tea.

From our first meeting with Mrs. Chang and Mr. Chou we all felt a warmth among us which is growing now into real friend-ships. Both are speaking quite freely now and for the first time the subjects include politics and religion, areas we never thought we could or would approach.

Mr. Chou still treads lightly with politics. He becomes under-stated when talking about Mao, the Revolution and liberation; but one can see he does so to keep himself in check out of respect for his new friends. We have no doubt that during his university days Mr. Chou was a loud and aggressive student leader. He is excitable and speaks quickly, a characteristic of the Cantonese. At one point in discussing religion he momentarily loses control and practically shouts, "Religion is rubbish, it is pure rubbish!"

Mrs. Chang presents her feelings and views in an effective, sincere manner which commands attention. At no time does she deprecate the United States, our people and our way of life. In fact she avoids doing so even in situations where she could have done with some good reason. She speaks with deep admiration for Chairman Mao and what he has done for the people of China. She compared the old China with India of today—illiterate, starving, dying masses. Her recollections from childhood, prior to the Revolution, include seeing people dying in the streets of Canton; the territorial sectioning of Shanghai when Western-owned parks had signs which read, "No dogs and Chinese al-lowed;" the prostitution, vice and corruption; and a runaway inflation that made money worthless. Her mother, she said, had to trade ten caddies of tea to obtain one caddie of much-needed salt. In the farm areas there were no flood controls, irrigation or fertilizer. Each had to scratch out a living usually below subsistence. "Today," she said, "China is developing and progressing. Our level of living is still low by Western standards, but all have jobs, food, clothing and medical attention. Our children are healthy, happy and well-educated. There is no prostitution, vice, theft or crime."

Whether one agrees with the system or not, there is no question that the force of Mao's personality and teachings have welded these remarkable people into a uniform, albeit regimented, group with discipline, productivity and a singleness of purpose. China is developing economically at a real growth rate of 8% to 10% annually. Everywhere we go progress is in evidence.

We extol our system and way of life as well and answer the many questions posed. The time passes quickly during this train ride and we all come away with an increased feeling of respect and friendship.

In Peking again we visit with Ambassador George Bush and present the Giant Panda Cub for the Embassy Art Collection.

We return to the Peking Hotel about 4:00 p.m. and rest awhile. At 6:30 we visit Ambassador George Bush at his living quarters, just ten minutes ride from our hotel. Ambassador Bush replaced Ambassador Bruce at the end of October. He is a young, energetic and talented diplomat whose career includes U.S. Ambassador to the United Nations and National Chairman of the Republican Party. Mrs. Bush was not present, having left for the U.S. the evening before with the visiting Dr. Henry Kissinger's group.

The Ambassador is fascinated with the account of our activities of the past few days and with the outstanding courtesies extended us. From our discussion it is obvious that the freedom of movement and activity we are enjoying are not possible at diplomatic and governmental levels. The Chinese must feel, as we do, that art transcends politics, language, race and religion.

We spend a pleasant hour with Ambassador Bush, then return to the hotel for a light dinner of beef casserole, rice and vegetables. We are to bed early, quite tired from the long day which began in Tangshan.

I arise early this morning, December 3, and have about half an hour before our usual departure time of 7:30. This provides an opportunity to witness the daily Chinese exercise called Tái Chi Quan. Chairman Mao's teachings stress the importance of good physical conditioning, and he has set the example many times in his heralded swims and walks. Old and young perform Tái Chi Quan when and where they have time, but at least each morning. Up and down the Boulevard of Peace I see thousands exercising, some individually, others in groups. The movements consist of stretching and bending in slow motion, maintaining tension in the working muscles, a kind of rudimentary ballet.

It is cold and clear, well below freezing. Mr. Chou had warned us the day before that we needed especially warm clothing to go to the Great Wall. The fact that it would be cold was emphasized by a howling wind that could be heard through the night. Fortunately we had purchased long woolen underwear, scarves and fur hats with ear covers. The long underwear of pure cashmere was purchased in the Friendship Store for $11 a set. With each passing day we all would agree it was the wisest purchase we made.

The subject of clothing is an interesting one. Prior to leaving the United States we had had considerable discussion about Mrs. Boehm's wardrobe. All advice (including mine) was that she should be understated with simple pants suits, modest colors, etc. She didn't accept this. She reasoned that she should be herself. She doubted that the Chinese would want her to change her clothing styles just as they wouldn't expect her to alter her character. Besides, her favorite and warmest coat is a sporting, thick, white mink. Unwilling to bow to the pressures, Mrs. Boehm called Mr. Chang at the Liaison Office and asked his advice. He said, "Why of course you should wear your white mink, Mrs. Boehm. We want you to be comfortable. Be yourself!"

So all through China Mrs. Boehm had her cashmeres under pants suits and her warm mink coat. Maurice and I had brought only lined raincoats and agreed many times that we weren't very smart.

It takes about two hours to drive by car to the Wall. The section visited is due north of the city. It is somewhat difficult driving because of the heavy flow of wagons, tractors and trucks coming from the farms. There is great activity and movement in the forms of trucks, cars, buses, bicycles, horse-drawn and mule-drawn wagons, motorcycles, three-wheel bikes and the usual military vehicles. For the first half of the trip the roads are excellent and straight. Small farms similar to our truck farms surround the city and Mr. Chou tells us they provide a good part of the food needs of Peking.

Just beyond the city are large underground caves in which fruit and vegetables are stored for winter consumption. The climate is dry and cool, perfect refrigeration. Among the traffic are many wagons carrying the city's daily needs of cabbage, apples, etc. We are surprised to see some cotton fields north of Peking, where the climate is about the same as that of Boston.

The flat plain around Peking suddenly ends as if truncated, and the hills begin. Our good road dwindles to narrow, perilous cliff-side passes as we're absorbed by the ranges. These Yinshan mountains are not high, perhaps a thousand meters at the fringe, but they are young and rugged, probably formed when the Himalayas made their convulsive appearance. The strata are sedimentary, mainly limestone, sandstone and clay.

Our first view of the Wall provides one of the most exciting moments of our entire trip. We can appreciate how important and impressive it is to the Chinese. It symbolizes the strength of the people, their determination and their defensive, rather than offensive, philosophy. Chairman Mao has told the young males that "they will become men when they go to the Wall." Mrs. Boehm's comment was, "I shall go to the Wall and become a person."

It appears we will be at the Wall in just a few minutes, but it is deceiving because of its size and serpentine nature. It is as if one is trying to follow an undulating snake through the hills. Now you see it, now you don't. Also adding to the confusion are a number of mini-walls traversing the same hills, built by landowners as additional protection against the bandit hordes from the north.

Finally we are there. As we open our car doors we are greeted by a biting 40 to 50 mile-an-hour wind and flurries of snow. It really is cold. The wind-chill factor could be 30 or 40 below zero. The top of the wall seems to serve as a channel for the winds and it is difficult to walk against it.

Sections of the Great Wall were completed during the Chin Dynasty (B.C. 221–206). Over the next three to four centuries the sections gradually were joined together forming an impenetrable barrier which, if straightened out, would be in excess of 4,000 miles, longer than our country is wide. It deteriorated over the centuries (most sections are in disrepair today) and was rebuilt in the Ming Dynasty by the Emperor Hung-wu (A.D. 1363–1399) after the last of the Yuan Dynasty Mongols were driven to the north. It is approximately 7 meters high, $5\frac{1}{2}$ meters thick and its top channel is as wide as a one-lane road. Apart from the protection it provided, the Chinese used the top of the wall as a raised highway on which people and goods moved constantly.

We walk about ¼ mile to the highest point of the wall. After snapping pictures quickly before our fingers freeze, we take to the sanctuary of our cars and start toward our second tour of the day, the great Ming Tombs. The Tombs are just about an hour's drive northwest of Peking (35 miles). Thirteen temples of the Ming Dynasty are set in a semi-circle around the Peking plain at the base of the suddenly-emerging hills. Each seems to be separated from the next by about a mile and they rise from the flat land in an impressive crescent.

Emperor Yung-Lo (A.D. 1403–1425) selected the sites for the tombs. The one we are to visit is the tomb of Wan-li. We are told the structure was completed in 1584, six years after it was begun.

The tomb of Wan-li is approached by a straight road lined by pine trees and monuments including life-size stone sculptures of elephants, lions, camels, tigers and dogs. This is the "sacred path" to the "hallowed" site. We walk through beautiful courtyards contained by carved stone walls and reach the mouth of the tomb. Six flights of steps take us down to the tomb floor and a large opening which originally was sealed by two marble doors a foot thick. Through the doors a main tunnel of impressive proportions leads to the burial room of the emperor. Two side tunnels lead to the burial chambers of his two empresses.

This particular tomb was excavated in 1958. Four tombs of the thirteen have yet to be located under their temples. The emperors did not want everyone to know the exact location of the burial rooms within their monuments because they didn't want their sarcophagi and treasures violated. Entrances to the tombs were hidden and sealed behind stone doors and walls measuring several meters thick. Slaves who provided the labor for the tombs were resigned to death, for their lips had to be sealed forever, 300 in the case of Wan-li. On the inside of each pair of doors was placed a heavy cement wedge that required an unusually strong man, or several, to move. These loyal subjects sealed themselves in and joined their royal patrons.

The Temple Museum above the tomb exhibits some of the riches found in the burial chambers—gold and silver garments, bronzes, red lacquer coffins, jewels, clothing, vessels of all precious materials and a variety of ceramics including celadon stonewares and feldspathic porcelains, blue and white pottery and porcelain and pottery with three-color lead glazes in yellow, purple and blue. Dominating the displays are murals, drawings and descriptions hailing the workers for their skills and achievements and deprecating the emperor for his cruelty and selfishness.

Before completing our tour we have a pleasant basket lunch in one of the curator's rooms. It consists of cold chicken, spam, cheese, small sandwiches, hard boiled eggs, pickles, apples, cookies and beer. Mr. Chou is giving us some of the history of the area. He and Mrs. Chang seem to alternate in this role. Somehow we are on the subject of fables and folk stories, which interest Mr. Chou. When he was a boy he had a great love of fables and read many of them. One in particular typifies their charm.

A very old man was walking along a country road. Suddenly he heard shouting and hollering over the hill. First to appear was a ferocious wolf who was running from many farmers who were trying to catch and kill him.

"Save me, please save me," said the wolf to the old man. "The farmers will kill me if they catch me!"

The old man was carrying a large empty sack. He set it on the ground, asked the wolf to hide in it and tied the top. The wolf lay perfectly still. When the farmers appeared they asked the old man if he had seen the wolf. He said he had not and they left; whereupon he untied the sack and let the wolf out.

The wolf looked at the old man and said, "I am very hungry from running so hard. I think I am going to eat you up."

"How can you do that!" exclaimed the old man. "I have just saved your life and now you want to eat me? That is not fair."

"Well, too bad," replied the wolf, "but that is what I think I should do."

"At least grant me this," said the old man. "Let's ask a few opinions to see if you are correct in wanting to eat me."

"All right," responded the wolf. "Here comes an old cow. Let's ask her."

The old man tells the old cow the story and asks if it is right that the wolf should eat him after having saved the wolf's life.

"Yes," said the old cow. "After all, look at what people are doing to me. For many years I have dutifully supplied milk for many families. Now that I am old and no longer can produce milk, I'm going to be killed and eaten. Is that fair? I think the wolf should eat you."

"See, what did I tell you?" happily crowed the wolf.

"But wait," protested the old man. "One opinion is not enough. Let's ask the old apple tree what he thinks."

The old apple tree had been listening to the story and, like the old cow, he was anxious to give his opinion.

"I agree with the old cow," said the old apple tree. "For forty years I have been providing delicious apples to feed several families. Now that I am old and no longer can produce apples, they will cut me down and use me for firewood. I think the wolf should eat you."

The wolf now was very happy and his mouth was watering. But the old man convinced him that they should have just one more opinion before the wolf ate him.

Down the road came an old farmer. The old man stopped him and related the story in detail. Then the old farmer asked that he be shown exactly what happened and how the wolf hid in the sack. The wolf obligingly jumped into the sack. The farmer quickly tied the top of the sack so the wolf could not escape, then pummelled the sack with his hoe and killed the wolf.

The old farmer then scolded the old man and said, "You see, you should never, for any reason, ever help a bad wolf."

As a good-natured exchange, Mrs. Boehm decides to relate to Mr. Chou and Mrs. Chang our fable of "Goldilocks and the Three Bears." The only trouble is she forgets how the story goes and looks to Maurice and me to provide the missing links. She didn't anticipate that we wouldn't remember either. The result is a hodgepodge of Goldilocks with bits of "Alice in Wonderland" and "Snow White and the Seven Dwarfs." Our friends have puzzled expressions through the whole exercise and smile politely at its end. We did little to advance the cause of American fables.

We drive back to Peking about 4:00 p.m. With two hours before dinner, we again visit the Friendship Store to buy more gifts. Between what we have been given and what we've purchased, we now have a mounting pile. We don't know how we'll get it all back to the States, but we're not worrying about it. How often can one come to China? And every item will have special meaning and recall happy memories.

Before the day ends we ask Mr. Chou and Mrs. Chang questions about living expenses. We are told that major family costs per month run about as follow: 15 yuan for food; 7 yuan for housing (including utilities, maintenance) ; 12 yuan for day care of children; 3.5 yuan for transportation. Medicine is free as are all services. Whatever is left over after necessities may be spent according to choice. And the choices are quite good, probably better than in Russia. The Chinese department stores carry a fair selection of merchandise. Or course, luxury items are few and quite expensive.

If there is money left over, one can open a savings account with the Bank of China with an earned interest rate of 2.7%. Automobiles are not privately owned; each governmental and civilian agency is assigned state cars according to its needs.

Prices for necessities have not changed since first established in 1949, and they are the same all over China. The people need not worry about inflation. The currency of China is the most stable in the world. As economic conditions continue to improve, so will the income and living standards.

There are some differences in costs for nonessential items in different cities and areas. But where costs are higher, incomes also are proportionally higher.

Relationships among the people are quite harmonious. Where problems do occur, they generally are settled with the help of others in the same neighborhood or working group. The whole society is organized, compartmentalized. The neighborhood revolutionary committee is the basic unit of organization. Led by a vice-chairman, it runs local schools, factories, and workshops and has the political responsibility of thoroughly converting all to socialism. The basic units of organization are called street committees which carry out the work to be done and arrange help for the old and ill, care for children, keep the neighborhood clean, set up study groups and political meetings, settle disputes and even conduct marriage counseling. The power vehicle for compliance is peer group pressure.

Some divorces occur. The street committee will attempt to mediate a couple's differences, very similar to Western group therapy. If the problems cannot be resolved, the couple will separate and share equally the children and property. If one child is involved, he will stay with the mother and be supported by the father.

Women marry at age twenty-five or older, men at age thirty. Other than as children, boys are always seen with boys, girls only with girls. I ask Mr. Chou what happens if two younger people fall in love, say at age nineteen? He says this cannot happen and would not be condoned. At this age a person must only be concerned with self-development, improving the mind, working for the state, and determining one's life work.

Mr. Chou states that premarital sex is practically unknown and that rape is rare. Adultery is harshly dealt with as it is considered a crime against the State; and homosexuality is equally abhorrent to the Chinese. Abortion is accepted so long as both husband and wife approve.

December 3rd ends with a light dinner of Chinese noodles with butter and cheese (a Chinese version of Fettuccini Alfredo) and delicious, thinly-sliced pork cutlets.

We are allowed to sleep a little later this morning, December 4, departing the hotel at 8:50. Fortunately we are conscious of being prompt. The Chinese always are. Wherever we've been our new hosts have been waiting outside their doors for our arrival, even in Tangshan when it was raining. Their preparation and coordination are thorough.

We are spending this morning at the Imperial Palaces (also called the Forbidden City), the largest and most complete group of ancient buildings which China has preserved to the present. They are so large and grand one can only give a sense of their scope and riches in art and architecture.

Like the Tombs, this complex was built in the Ming Emperor Yung Lo's reign. In later periods there were reconstruction and restoration, as needed. It occupies an entire area of 720,000 square meters with over 9,000 rooms, each of which is an individual marvel of construction.

We are told by our guide, a bright young lady named Yang Yu-Liang (which means "fine jade") that Emperor Yung Lo brought together on the site 10,000 of China's best architects, artists, masons, medalists, carpenters and ceramists for this monumental project. About eleven years were needed to build the City.

The Palaces are divided into two parts. Front buildings were used for state business, meetings and the issuance of edicts and decrees. Rear parts were for living quarters, study and leisure pursuits. This was the center of political power and rule during the Ming and Ching Dynasties.

Chinese love beautiful, romantic names. Some of the Palace names are "Hall of Supreme Harmony," "Hall of Preserving Harmony," "Palace of Heavenly Purity," "Hall of Union," "Palace of Earthly Tranquility," "Hall of Royal Peace," "Hall of Mental Cultivation," "Hall of Absolute," "Hall of Manifest Origin," "Palace of Gathering Excellence."

The Imperial gardens are magnificent, covering an area of approximately 7,000 square meters. Pines and cypresses 400 years old are carefully preserved. A primary feature of the gardens is

Outside the spectacular Imperial Palaces are large gold-leafed bronze sculptures and huge 5000-pound bronze pots, as seen above the courtyard in the photo below.

the limestone conglomerate rocks which are everywhere. This was one of the most inspiring areas for Maurice Eyeington. He took out his sketch pad and quickly conceived a rough design incorporating the ancient Dragon's Claw Tree with the spectacular Red-billed Blue Magpie, a magnificent bird we saw in great numbers around Peking. This would later be translated into one of the more important sculptures issued by our Trenton studio (*see color plate*).

In addition to indoor sculpture there are countless outdoor sculptures, mainly gilded bronzes of immense scale; and huge bronze pots which weigh about 5,000 pounds surround the Palaces. These are placed every fifty feet or so. Each was gilded with about five pounds of gold! The pots were kept filled with water for immediate use in case of fire in one of the Palaces.

In the "Hall of Union" we see two unique clocks. One, the clepsydra, is a water clock which records time by the dripping of water, on the same principle as the sand hour clock. The clepsydra is man's oldest timepiece. It was used by the ancient Chinese 2500 years ago. The second clock is a mechanical striking one built by craftsmen of the Imperial Household of Emperor Chia Ch'ing in 1797.

The most impressive carving in the Palaces is the "Dragon Pavement," a finely-sculptured solid block of marble approximately 75 feet long, 10 feet wide, 5 feet thick. It weighs 500,000 pounds, and is placed in the central stairwell of the "Hall of Preserving Harmony," built in the Ming period. How was such a gigantic stone moved from the mountains to Peking? No one, not even the emperor, was allowed to use this stairwell. It was reserved exclusively for ancestral spirits of the royal families.

Of greatest interest to us, of course, are the porcelain collections of the Forbidden City, a grand chronological display which begins with excavated pottery from about 4,000 B.C. Two hours here is little time to spend. One can trace the development of pottery, stoneware and porcelain quality, design, glazes and color through magnificent specimens, about 1,000 pieces total. The most interesting piece in the collection is a large two-handled urn about 36″ tall and 24″ in diameter, which combines most of the glazing and enameling techniques of Chinese porcelain history. It is sectioned into areas of underglaze blue and red, overglaze *famille verte* and *famille rose*, underglaze blue and white with overglaze enamels, celadon-colored slip, hidden decoration, sgraffito and reserve decoration.

Before leaving the Imperial Palaces we are graciously received by the Director, Mr. Wong Ching-fu, an impeccably attired, refined man. We enjoy tea and conversation in one of the rooms of the "Palace of Gathering Excellence," living quarters of the empresses and imperial concubines of the Ming and Ching courts. Mrs. Boehm presents Mr. Wong with a "Bird of Peace" plate for the porcelain collections. Mr. Wong returns the gesture by presenting Mrs. Boehm with two excellent books on the porcelains in the Palaces. As with other recipients of the plate, and also the book, Mr. Wong is effusive in his gratitude. The importance and significance of the "Bird of Peace" sculpture and book presentations to Chairman Mao by former President Nixon are understood.

Mr. Wong adds some interesting facts about the Palaces. In 1911 Sun Yat Sen and the people overthrew the last of the Ching Emperors, Hsuan Tung, and for the first time the front half of the City was open to the people. Up to this time no one but the royal families, commissioners, advisors, guards and royal staff could enter. In 1925 the rear part of the Palaces was opened as well. Up until the October 1, 1949 Revolution, the Palaces were in a state of disrepair. Extensive restoration has been going on since then under the China Conservation Bureau, an organization which named and now maintains 180 national monuments. Among these are the Palaces, the Great Wall, and the Ming Tombs.

Mr. Wong explains that much of the art and furniture presently in the Imperial Palaces gradually have been built back into collections over the last twenty-five years. We are told that when Chiang Kai-shek fled China in 1949, he took with him to Taiwan

2300 large casks filled with the art treasures of the Forbidden City.

On leaving Mr. Wong and the Palaces, we take a few moments to drive around Tien An Men Square, just outside the Heavenly Peace Gates. Here is where Chairman Mao addressed the people on the day of liberation. The square is immense, covering about 100 acres. One can easily visualize a million people gathering in this area.

On one side of the square is the Great Hall, where, we were told in Washington, the Mute Swans sculpture is placed. Our hosts cannot confirm this and it is not possible to enter the Hall.

At the center of the square facing the Boulevard of Peace are large color photographs of Marx and Engels on the left, of Lenin and Stalin on the right. They appear to be about twelve feet square. The centrally-placed photo of Mao is larger.

We take two hours for lunch and rest back at the hotel, then

Carving a horse figure on a wood block for printing.

spend a pleasant afternoon at the "Glorious Treasures Studio" which is devoted strictly to woodblock printing. This is a fascinating art begun around A.D. 900 in the Tang Dynasty.

The Director, Mr. Mei Su-chia, first receives us for tea and cigarettes and we exchange small gifts. We then see some of the outstanding work of the studio, prints of paintings that require as many as 1300 printing blocks. Block printing is entirely a hand art. The wood carvers must reduce a painting to sections and colors, a carved block for each. The process requires precise planning and cutting. Pear wood is used.

Each block later will be inked by hand to receive the print paper which must be perfectly positioned, then laid over the block. The ink is transferred by rubbing and pressing the paper against the block. In the case of the print with 1300 blocks, this procedure had to be repeated 1300 times.

We are fascinated to learn that the number of each print is

Wood block printing. Some prints are pressed hundreds of times over the inked blocks.

limited and that they are sold on that basis. The Chinese have been practicing the concept of limited editions for many years.

Mr. Mei takes us on a tour of the studio. One hundred eighty artists and craftsmen work on the prints, a mixture of very young to very old as we've seen in all of the art studies. Prior to completing our visit we are allowed to purchase a selection of fine pieces.

We have an interesting experience at the Friendship Store on the way back to our hotel. The day before, Mrs. Boehm wanted to purchase a miniature bottle painting that, incredibly, has 100 people in the design. The clerk wouldn't sell it because it was slightly damaged. But the clerk promised to check with the director and suggested we call back the following day. We do. Without having requested it, Mrs. Boehm receives the painting at a discount of $33\frac{1}{3}\%$.

During the day we continue to enjoy our close friendship with Mrs. Chang and Mr. Chou. Mrs. Chang highly complimented Mrs. Boehm by saying she was very fond of her and expressed the hope that she might be Helen Boehm's friend for life. Mrs. Boehm has caught the tempo of the people now and in her inimitable fashion is making friends everywhere she goes. She wants to have a picture taken with every group of children she sees. She hugs and kisses them and all seem to respond immediately to her warmth and friendship. She is a remarkable person.

One young lady asks if they might be photographed together, something we never expected would happen. After the photo there is more hugging and kissing. "Friendship, friendship, American friends," over and over again it is repeated by all we meet. And it is sincere. After almost a week here, Mrs. Boehm, Maurice and I agree that these are the most gracious, hospitable and kindly people we've ever met.

We have our last dinner at the Peking Hotel. At our request it is a repeat of the night before. We retire early as we must be ready to depart for the airport at 7:00 a.m.

The next morning, December 5, the bell men help us with our

Helen Boehm makes friends with Chinese children in the Imperial Palace courtyard.

luggage. One fellow in particular who asked that we call him "Sammy" is very sorry to see us leave. He is a happy chap with a perpetual smile and all week long in his limited English he called us his "good American friends." We offer him and the others (all seem to be in their late teens) a five-pound box of Turkish Delight jellies. The other boys quickly refuse as they are counseled not to accept gifts or gratuities; but when we explain to Sammy it is simply candy from the West to mark our friendship, he explains to the others that it will be all right.

When we get down to the lobby we are delighted to see Counsellor Hu of the Association. He arose early to accompany us to the airport and see us off on the balance of our journey.

At Peking Airport we board a new Trident jet recently purchased by China from England. There is a first-class section but no one occupies it. (The Chinese refer to first and second class as "soft" and "hard.") They do not like to make class distinctions. We are glad we are joining the passengers in the rear section. All but one seat is filled. The flight to Hangchow (Che Kiang Province) is about one and one-half hours. Tea and candy are served. Printed messages in the plane are both in English and Chinese. For our benefit (we are the only foreigners on board) all announcements by the stewardesses are repeated in English.

Basketweaving in the West Lake Bamboo Factory.

CHAPTER IX

Hangchow

THERE IS NO specific reason for going to Hangchow. Flights within China are not daily; and in that we have to spend two days somewhere to make our connections to Nanchang and Ching-te-Chen, our hosts thought we should spend them in the "Garden City" of China. On departing Peking Mr. Hu's final remarks are, "You will like Hangchow. About it the Chinese people say, 'In the heavens there is a paradise; on earth there is Hangchow.'"

Hangchow Airport is new and modern with the ever-present photo of Mao on the terminal building. This time three cars are waiting for us. Apparently Mr. Chou warned our hosts here of our rapidly increasing luggage. In Peking we bought three additional large pieces, all of which already are full. Our hosts from the Association in Hangchow are Mr. Lu Ho-sen and Mr. Chao Chia-fu.

Hangchow is an old city whose known history dates back about 2100 years. It lies on the western corner of a large spring-fed lake. Low hills surround the lake on three sides. "West Lake," as it is called, has an area of 6 km. and a shoreline of about 15 km. Causeways divide the lake into three parts. The lake is circled almost entirely by parks that are maintained year-round by a staff of 3,000 workers. Two of the park names are "Orioles Singing in the Willows" and "Autumn Moon on the Calm Lake." The surrounding hills are well known for their famous springs, such as "Dragon Well" and their outstanding growths of Lung Chin green tea. On the way from the airport our hosts have us driven through some of the parks. Even cold and dreary weather cannot dim the beauty of this magnificent city.

The warm and friendly people of Hangchow, on the banks of West Lake.

In the warmer seasons, we are told, as many as 40,000 persons from all over China swell the population of Hangchow. It is a resort where workers and their families come to rest and enjoy. The train ride from Shanghai is about 200 km. which costs 3 yuan, round trip. Accommodations average 1 yuan a day and food is about the same. A person from Shanghai could travel to and from Hangchow and spend seven days for a total cost of 16 yuan ($8.00).

The people of Hangchow have a somewhat different look about them than those of Peking. Complexions are fairer, some women wear colored garments, and everyone seems to move at a more relaxed pace.

One immediately noticeable difference in the way of life is the complete absence of horses and mules. These people move all the lighter materials (and some heavy) in carts they pull themselves. Heaviest materials are moved by barges and boats on the multitude of waterways.

The presence of Mao and his teachings, however, are just as obvious and prevalent. And Hangchow has the same methods of every town and city of getting messages and news to the people. A network of loudspeakers that cover the town on a grid system carries alternating music (mainly Peking operas) and political statements. Large bulletin boards carry world news which is posted daily in the form of communiqués.

Speaking of communiqués, while having breakfast the morning of our departure from Peking we met Mr. Sam Jaffe, a reporter for the Chicago Daily News. He has been an Asia correspondent since the Korean War and has reported for the *New York Herald-Tribune*, *Life* Magazine and ABC and CBS news. Mr. Jaffe made the original trip with former President Nixon and has returned several times since. He is the first American newsman permitted to travel widely in China this year.

He told us the communiqué issued a few days ago about Dr. Kissinger's trip to China (which ended last Monday, December 1) was discouragingly short, only six lines long. The only good news was that President Ford planned to visit China the next year. Mr. Jaffe said that he and others of the foreign press corps felt that Chinese-American relations were currently at a low point. They attributed this to the appointment of George Bush as our Ambassador (whose conservative bent might not be to the liking of the Chinese), and to the suddenness of the change from former Ambassador David Bruce, apparently without prior consultation with the Chinese.

Mr. Jaffe was pleased to hear of the warmth and hospitality given us, adding that his experience had been the same over the last two years. Like us he had fallen in love with China and its people. He felt that in spite of who the diplomats are and what they do, Chinese-American friendship would continue to move forward. The Chinese people have never lost their warm feelings toward Americans. What is needed, said Mr. Jaffe, and we agree, are a lot more exchanges of people other than diplomats.

On the plane flying in, Mrs. Chang continues to answer any

questions posed by Mrs. Boehm. She speaks about Lin Piao's divisive actions and his leanings toward Russia, thus his fall from power. She explains something else we are curious about. We keep hearing, or reading the statement, "Learn from Tachai for agriculture."

Mrs. Chang explains that there are several outstanding examples of self-reliance, success stories so to speak, that Chairman Mao constantly refers to in setting goals for the people. Tachai is a farming village that for years was beset with problems including annual flooding, hunger, disease, and overall poverty. After the Revolution the government offered to help Tachai by sending in agronomists, engineers, etc. But the people were so imbued with Mao's teachings of self-reliance they proudly refused help and determined to pull themselves up by their own bootstraps. And they did. Through teamwork and cooperation they built dams and levees for flood control, terraced and irrigated the fields, rebuilt their homes and farms and even beautified their village by planting thousands of trees and plants.

The industrial example Mao refers to is Taching. We are not told the specifics but apparently the people of this oil-producing village made similar strides. The complete exhortation by Mao on high goals is, "Learn from Tachai for agriculture; learn from Taching for industry. The whole country learns from the People's Liberation Army. And the Army learns from the people."

We arrive at the Hangchow Hotel about 10:30 a.m. On entering our rooms we realize that there is no heat and it is our misfortune to be here during an unusual cold spell. The temperature outside is about 35°. In our rooms it is 40°, and for this day and night it won't get any warmer. At lunch we meet an English-speaking French couple who had plans to stay three days; but one night in the cold rooms has them packing to leave. Well, we do have some scotch and vodka left, and the cashmere longjohns. Besides, the people of Hangchow endure it and all seem very healthy.

Mr. Lu and Mr. Chao are outstanding hosts, former teachers who now head the Association of Hangchow. Mr. Lu is especially

Amid the beautiful scenery of West Lake.

ebullient and friendly, always putting his arm around one of us as we walk, or locking arms with us. Both are proud of the American friends they've made, especially the visit here of Senators Hugh Scott and Mike Mansfield. James Reston, the columnist, and other members of the U.S. press have been here. Recently a group of professors from Michigan University were guests.

In the afternoon we are treated to a sight-seeing tour of this picturesque city. First a covered cabin (thank goodness!) boat ride around West Lake, then a walk through some of the parks. All are reflective of Chinese grace and design, a softly blended mélange of trees, flowers, winding paths, sculpture, waterways and open red-lacquered pavilions.

Our dinner is excellent, a whole carp basted with sweet and sour sauces, fried shrimp, chicken soup, pork and mushrooms, rice and oranges. As usual we retire early, about 9:00 p.m. The rooms are so cold we have to leave our heavy underwear and sweaters on. Blankets are plentiful and, after the initial shock, my bed warms up. Actually it proved to be one of our best night's sleep and the following day we already seem inured to the cold.

We are looking forward this morning, December 6, to visiting the local bamboo factory. We had hoped to visit one of the many silk factories for which Hangchow is famous but they are not very active this time of year and the main plant (or model plant) is undergoing extensive renovation.

The director of the West Lake Bamboo Ware Factory is Mr. Chang, Jen-Kuei, a quite elderly man who has worked with bamboo all his life, as did his parents and grandparents. We are told by Mr. Lu that Mr. Chang was illiterate but his work and leadership qualities were so outstanding that he was sent to Peking for administrative and political training and some schooling.

It is amazing what these people can do with bamboo. In the exhibition room over tea and cigarettes we are treated to a variety of shapes and colors that defy description. Decorative and utilitarian pieces, animal reproductions with precise character and color, bamboo reproductions of bronze and porcelain sculptures, bowls and vases.

The factory employs 198 people. Prior to forming this cooperative in 1954, all work was done at home by fourteen different families working and selling independently. Production was small and inefficient and there was little selection. Each family had its own specialty. Since formation of the factory, others have been trained and production has risen dramatically. The selection now includes 240 different ornamental subjects and forty functional furniture pieces. Like all factories in the light industries, a percentage of production is committed for export. Forty-five percent of the staff are female. All bamboo used is grown in this province (Che Kiang).

Working conditions in the factory are good, although in all buildings there is no heat. Most of the work, including materials preparation, is done by hand. The tools used are ingenious. Large hammers made of heavy, telescoped bamboo pieces, chisels with

At the bamboo factory we saw workers putting the natural tools of the body to use. This man wears felt shoes so that he may steady the bamboo with his feet as he works with it. *Below*, a friendly demonstration by one of the female members of the staff, who comprise 45% of the factory's work force.

bamboo handles, simple drills constructed of bamboo and rope that turn the bits with an alternating spring-like action, metal forms of different kinds for stripping the bamboo into various thin shapes (round, flat, square, triangular, etc.), and use of the natural tools of the body. Most wear felt shoes so they may steady or grip the bamboo with the feet when working with it. And tearing of the material into strips is aided with the teeth. The weavers' hands move so quickly they are almost a blur.

We thoroughly enjoy the bamboo factory and, after an exchange of small gifts, are taken downtown for shopping. This is another of the really pleasant experiences of the trip. There is no Friendship Store in Hangchow (one is under construction) so we are taken into the town shops. A crowd gathers everywhere we go and we are greeted with constant smiles, waves and handshakes. The shopkeepers are gracious and all prices are posted. We spend at least an hour in the silk shop selecting brocaded pure silk at $5 to $6 a yard. We wonder how the people can afford even this much for the most beautiful silks. We are told that brocades are purchased rarely, only for special occasions— marriages, holiday-wear, etc.

Among the silks we purchase are several in a magnificent Imperial jade color. Mr. Chou points out that this special color once was reserved exclusively for the Emperors' families.

We are brought back to the hotel for lunch and rest from 12:00 to 2:00. As usual we eat too much, but everything seems good. We are particularly enjoying the beer. We think it is comparable to the best Western beers.

While lunching, an attractive nineteen-year-old lady comes to our table and introduces herself as "Jo" in perfect English. She is a student at Hangchow University and is majoring in English and political science. She plans to be a teacher. With less than two years of study in English, Jo speaks remarkably well. Her purpose in coming to the table is to ask if we would speak with her for a while so she may improve her English. Later she brings her classmate over and we have a friendly talk. The girls promise to correspond with us.

After lunch we are taken to the local museum where we spend about an hour viewing a well-displayed collection of artifacts and early pottery and porcelain.

Next we visit two memorable monuments. The first is a Buddhist Temple built about 1600 years ago. It is a huge closed structure about 125 feet high. It serves only to house a giant wooden Buddha. One is truly startled at the size and ornateness of the great Buddha. It sits on a large twenty-foot-tall base decorated with a lotus leaf motif. From the base the figure rises an additional sixty feet. It was constructed from twenty-four large pieces of wood. Around the walls are dozens more large wooden sculptures (each about twice the size of a big man) that represent the Buddha's priests and students.

This painted wooden Buddha in Hangchow rises eighty feet in the air and sculptures of his priests and students tower above us.

The second monument is the Liu Ho Pagoda of Six Harmonies (mind, body, speech, opinion, abstinence from temptation, and wealth) which is over 1,000 years old. It rises above the Chien Tang River about 190 feet. Its construction is completely of wood. Thirteen levels comprise the exterior; seven stories or floors are on the interior.

Our second day in Hangchow is coming to an end. We will be sorry to leave this piece of paradise and these friendly people. We all hope we can return again in the spring or fall when Hangchow is at its most beautiful.

Our final dinner in Hangchow consists of baked carp, black fungus with peas, shredded pork with onions and mushrooms, an outstanding egg and tomato soup, rice, oranges and tea. After dinner we are visited a few moments by Mr. Lu. On behalf of the Friendship Association he presents each of us with a silk painting bearing a printed photo of Hangchow.

Mr. Chao and Mr. Lu meet us at the hotel in the morning (December 7) to escort the four of us to the airport. We are embarrassed when we see a small Army personnel carrier with the two cars. It was arranged for our luggage. Since the start of the trip we have now purchased four new large pieces and they all are full. We keep promising each other that we'll do no more buying, but when we see beautiful art and handicrafts our resolve weakens. The gifts we continue to receive at each point also help to fill new bags.

We are halfway through our trip and we've already been exposed to thirteen of the outstanding arts and crafts of China. The nine listed in the section describing our visit to the Peking Fine Arts and Handicraft Company, ceramics of Tangshan, wood block printing, silk weaving and needlework and bamboo.

While waiting for our plane to leave Hangchow we discover Chinese perfume in the airport shop. One brand, made from the scent of roses, is available and is very pleasant.

We board our plane at 9:30 a.m., a Russian propeller-driven Illyushin, a pretty good craft. It is lumbering, but it seems quieter and smoother than the old Fairchilds (which are similar). The flight to Nanchang is about 250 miles, requiring one hour and ten minutes. All but one seat on the plane is filled. Again we are the only foreigners on board.

The flight becomes a lot of fun when Mrs. Boehm decides to walk the aisles and make friends with the passengers, with the help of Mrs. Chang. All the way to Nanchang she's teaching the Chinese phrases like, "I like beer," "I like candy," "How are you?" and "I am fine." She has the whole plane repeating them in unison and there is much good-natured fun and friendship. Baroness Von Trapp transported to China! Add about forty-five more Chinese friends. Maurice is pinioned in the seat behind me. At 6'6" there is not enough leg room in the Illyushin.

In Nanchang we are greeted by two Association members, Mr. Ho Shih-ching and Mrs. Hu So-ying. Three cars are waiting to take us on the long journey to Ching-te-Chen. But first we will have lunch at the airport. It is delicious, much spicier than what we've had in Peking, Tangshan and Hangchow. It consists of baked carp, shredded cabbage, chicken, egg and vegetable soup, beef, steamed bread dough, rice, beer and apples. Lots of garlic and, for the first time, very hot chili pepper.

Mr. Ho tells us a little about Nanchang during lunch. It and Ching-te-Chen are in the province of Kiangsi. Like most of the provinces, the people are Han (90% of the entire population of China is Han, although the Chinese count about fifty-four nationalities in their country.) Nanchang and the surrounding areas are best known for rice, cotton, sugar, fertilizer, tobacco, Mandarin oranges and pears. Six million square acres are devoted to agriculture, close to five million to rice alone. The body of water we flew over coming into Nanchang is Poyong Lake, one of the largest in China. It swells to 2700 square miles during the monsoon season.

CHAPTER X

Ching-te-Chen,
Mecca of Fine Porcelain

BEFORE BEGINNING our Ching-te-Chen adventure, it is interesting to consider the city as it was during the height of Western influence, early in the 18th century. It must be remembered that the city was sacked and destroyed several times as the tides of power moved with the changing dynasties. Yet each rebuilding only slightly altered its character and we will see that few changes have been made since 1949.

In the year 1712 Père d'Entrecolles, a Jesuit missionary, visited Ching-te-Chen and wrote a detailed description of what he saw. At the time the factories were producing tremendous quantities of porcelain for the insatiable West. Father d'Entrecolles wrote of the city as it appeared when he arrived at night: "The sight with which one is greeted on entering through one of the gorges consists of volumes of smoke and flame rising in different places, so as to define all the outlines of the town. Approaching at nightfall, the scene reminds one of a city in flames."

Père d'Entrecolles estimated there were three thousand kilns operating year-round, eighteen thousand families of potters, and a total population of one million. The customary protective walls were not built around Ching-te-Chen in order to allow continuing rapid growth outward and to facilitate the movement of tremendous quantities of raw materials in and porcelains out. To further ease the traffic of hand-drawn carts and shoulder racks carrying their precious cargoes, planners of the city constructed buildings on blocks with streets at right angles to one another, very similar to a modern American city.

Because of its open structure, Ching-te-Chen had heavy security at all times. A mandarin ruled with the aid of block chiefs and an average of one guard per building. Rich merchants lived in grand homes, but there were few. Father d'Entrecolles describes the majority of the people as destitute and illiterate; compensation in the porcelain works was low; and the commercial success of the city attracted the rural poor, weak and sick who came in search of alms and work.

Within this modest historical framework, we begin our journey to Ching-te-Chen in our three-car caravan. Mr. Ho and Mrs. Yu are making the trip with us, so we now have a party of seven as well as our luggage. The distance is only about 150 miles but it will take five hours to drive through rather rugged country with no paved roads. In Peking Mr. Hu warned us to be prepared for a difficult trip. In fact, a year ago when we asked if we might visit Ching-te-Chen, the liaison office in Washington said they thought it would not be possible. After all, no American has set foot in the ancient porcelain city since long before the second World War. When we were told on arrival in China that arrangements had been made for us to see Ching-te-Chen, we were immensely pleased and honored. We will be going back 2,000 years to the birthplace of fine porcelain. Only a handful of Westerners ever have been there.

As soon as we leave Nanchang we are on unpaved road. The soil is a bright red clay similar to the Brunswick shale that runs from Connecticut through New Jersey to Virginia. At first the land is flat and our route stretches out before us like an endless red snake. Immediately we begin to see rice fields interspersed with small, elevated plots of corn, cabbage, sugar cane, sweet potatoes and tomatoes. Close to the road are brick kilns, large mounds of soil and clay about the size of a small house, with smoking chimneys. From a distance they look like a series of burning sand dunes or bee hives.

People are everywhere in the fields, from little children to the elderly, preparing the earth for the coming spring planting. Two rice crops a year are harvested. The present interlude is the time to clean irrigation channels, build new fields, repair equipment and tidy up things.

Animals are plentiful, especially the important water buffalo. It is essential to the people because it is the only beast of burden which can function in this land of water and mud; and it also provides milk and meat. Pigs are equally prevalent. They seem to be all over the fields and roads. Oftentimes we see a sow and seven or eight frolicking piglets walking the side of the road unattended. Other animals in abundance are geese, ducks and chickens. More than once we stop to let a gaggle of geese go by.

The road is difficult to drive. It is narrow with sloping shoulders. When an occasional truck or tractor comes toward us, the drivers stay in the middle to the last moment, then peel off right and left, giving up as little road as they have to. It is raining lightly, making the red clay quite slippery. To compound the difficulties, the farmers place large stones the size of a football about four feet from the edge of the road and on both sides. Spacing between them is about fifty feet. This is to force cars and trucks to the center to prevent them from tearing up the shoulders where the hand-drawn carts must go.

All along the route men and boys are endlessly working on the road, carrying new soil and stones to repair potholes. At times we would come upon a long row of them pushing soil back on the road with flat, horizontal hoes. Having done this for years in some cases, they seem to ignore the vehicles as they pass. They thrust the hoe forward as we approach, then withdraw it just as we are about to ride over it. The rhythm isn't broken.

Drivers in China lean on their horns constantly. We don't know why. No one seems to pay much attention. Our driver starts blowing his horn about 500 feet before we come upon a wagon or pedestrian, and he keeps on blowing it as we pass. When he comes up behind another car or truck, he starts his horn and continues until he gets by. This can take a while as the road is too narrow for passing in some sections. Maurice and I are driving the car in spirit all the way from the rear seat. We can't believe we'll get through the trip without an accident. Horns are blowing and people, pigs, chickens and geese scatter everywhere.

Mr. Ho, one of the more expressive friends we've met, seems particularly annoyed if we are held up by another vehicle. When we finally ease past unyielding drivers, we notice he opens his window and raises one, two or three fingers at them. We are reluctant to ask him the significance of these gestures, so later we question Mr. Chou about it. He laughs and says, "He raises one finger when he is annoyed; two fingers when he is mad; three fingers when he is very mad."

About half way to Ching-te-Chen we stop at a roadside country hotel for a break and some hot tea. Adults and children gather around our cars. It is doubtful that any of them ever have seen an American, or even a Westerner. At first their curiosity is cautious; but by the time we leave they are smiling and waving. Before departing we visit the outdoor, roofless latrine. The wind is strong and finally I am certain of the purpose of the hood at one end of the trench.

As we approach Ching-te-Chen we leave the flat rice plains and the hills begin to rise. Still, wherever low wet ground exists there are rice beds. Each hill is terraced for planting other crops, forming a striated symmetrical collar around the valleys. The road becomes increasingly hazardous and narrows as we go. The rain seems to be heavier. In a few areas the mud is so thick we don't think we'll get through. The lead car is momentarily mired on one occasion.

Finally the road broadens and is paved again as we enter Ching-te-Chen. It was a rough trip but worth the experience that we know will be rare and rewarding.

On our eventual return to the United States the discomforts we endured in reaching Ching-te-Chen will seem minor in com-

parison to those encountered by foreign visitors just a few decades before. Shortly after our trip to China we received by mail
another personal account of a visit to the porcelain center from
Mr. James L. Howe, Jr. of Lexington, Virginia, who had read
a press article of our trip. Mr. Howe is an educator who spent
three years at the Mission College of Hangchow developing
courses in industrial chemistry. In the summer of 1924 he
traveled to Ching-te-Chen with a Mr. Pond, one of his Chinese
students. We can't include here the entire report; but Mr. Howe's
description of the three and a half day trip from Nanchang to
Ching-te-Chen, the 150 miles or so we covered by car in five
harrowing hours, vividly portrays the isolation of the city and
allows a glimpse of its poverty and backwardness during the
1920s. Mr. Howe confirms the living conditions as reported by
Père d'Entrecolles more than two hundred years before.

Mr. Howe wrote, "It was the writer's rare privilege to make a
visit to this most interesting interior Chinese city during the
summer of 1924, this trip being the most outstanding of experiences had in three years of life in China. Many times this city
with its reputation of a porcelain center had come to my attention, and as far back as 1920 I had read an extremely interesting article in the *National Geographic* Magazine entitled
'The World's Ancient Porcelain Center.' Our poet, Longfellow,
makes mention in his 'Keramos' of the burning town of Kintehchen!

"The city of Kintehchen is not, according to the Chinese, a
city, but a 'chen' or unwalled town. It is situated in Kiangsi
Province near the border of Anwei, and relatively only a short
distance from the capital city of Nanchang. Its inaccessibility is
the reason for its being so little known, and so rarely visited by
the foreigner. Kintehchen owing to its isolation is also one of the
most conservative and backward of the larger Chinese cities.
With a population variously estimated at from one half to one
million souls it is almost unbelievable that there are no newspapers, water systems, modern schools or hospitals, while the

only means of transportation, other than walking, is the few rickshas that are allowed to operate only at specified hours during the day. It has been said that the great hindrance to development lies in the hostile feeling of its citizens to foreigners and their customs, but in the writer's opinion, speaking after four days spent under the hospitality of certain of its men, this belief is most emphatically fallacious. The people have not had a chance to obtain even a taste of our modern civilization, and were this given them there is no doubt in my mind but that they would accept with relish any development that would make for a better life for her hundreds of thousand inhabitants.

"It was on a broiling hot day in July, one found only in an interior province of Central China, that in company with one of my students, I took the train which runs between Kiukiang and Nanchang. The distance between these cities is but seventy miles, and the schedule running time is eight hours. However our train was unable to conform to such a rapid schedule, and it took us over nine hours to make the run. Arrived in Nanchang we had some difficulty with the ever present police and soldiers, who keep a very close check on any foreigner who strays so far into the interior. However after my passport had been examined, and numerous of my visiting cards had been dispensed with, we were allowed to proceed to the Y.M.C.A. that we had heard was available for visitors. All coolies of whatever dialect know the words 'Chin Neah Wei,' and these brought us quickly to the welcome Y. Here we located a very accommodating English-speaking clerk who told us we could be provided with food but that they had no dormitory accommodations. The latter was rather disappointing news, for after our hard trip we were both pretty tired, and bed sounded even better than food. However we were told that our 'pu kais' (bedding) could be placed upon the floor of one of the school rooms, so we immediately began our preparations for the night. One may imagine with what pleasure we soon afterward saw a foreigner enter the building. He turned out to be the foreign secretary of the Y and welcomed us most cordially, insisting on our removing to his home for the night. Never did a real bed and a cold bath feel so good.

"Early the next morning we were off on our way by small launch which carried us the fifteen miles down river to the great Poyong Lake. We were headed for the city of Raochow which is on one arm of the lake, and it was a long ten hours trip, as part of the time we had to move very slowly to avoid grounding in the shallow parts of the lake. In ordinary weather in a more uncongested boat the trip would have been one of indescribable beauty, but never was a sun so scorching hot or a small boat so completely packed with human cargo.

"When eventually we arrived at Raochow at about eight o'clock that night we were quite fatigued. I had but one thought and that was to hire our houseboat and be off for the trip up the beautiful clear river which I had been told was delightful for swimming. One in China ordinarily takes his life in his hand when making use of river water, unboiled, for any purpose, even for bathing. This Beh Geang or North River, however, is a rare exception, having the reputation of being without great pollution. That reputation was sufficient, for the way I was feeling I was glad enough later to have a cool swim, even though it was running some risk.

"After bargaining for a houseboat for our trip up river to Kintehchen, and being held up unmercifully because the news had gone out that a foreigner was in the neighborhood and wished a boat, we finally succeeded in getting our crew assembled. At last we thought that we were off, but at the customs and police stations we were again forced to make a halt for questioning. However here we received the greatest of courtesy, they even offering us an armed guard to make the trip. After a little consideration we thought it unnecessary, so with the good wishes of the officers we were really off.

"It was not until eleven that we left the Lake and entered the North River, but a brisk breeze had sprung up and it was much cooler. However the cool clear water, with the path of a full moon out across it, was irresistible, and in less time than it takes to tell I was in the water and swimming along by the slow moving boat. I should like to know of the thoughts of those boatmen, for I could hear them commenting on the strange ways of the 'foreign devils.' I really think they were worried lest I should drown and they lose their rich fare. That hour's swim will always be a memory sweet to me. Never did one sleep more peacefully than I that night even though lying on hard boards and being roughly tossed by the constant jerk of the paddle that ceased not during all the night.

"The next day was another of sweltering heat, but after a hearty breakfast consisting of rice and eggs, cooked by our boatmen, and a couple of cups of G. Washington coffee, the only food that we carried with us, we were ready for another swim. All that day we pushed on up stream, the crew only resting from their constant paddling by getting ashore and pulling the boat along. We were going against a fairly rapid current, and with no breeze to use the sails with which all houseboats are equipped, our progress was indeed slow. However it was not an unpleasant life, for the countless villages that we passed were interesting and stopping at them to obtain our supplies broke the monotony, and in addition the swimming was always delightfully refreshing. My student and I were both well supplied with reading material, and many hours were enjoyed at this. Thus for three days we travelled, and on the afternoon of the fourth we saw one of the most remarkable sights I ever beheld. It was the innumerable smoking chimneys of a great industrial city here in this most isolated of regions.

"The current of the river just below the city was exceedingly strong, so that no progress could be made by paddling. It was necessary for two of our crew to go ashore with ropes and pull, while the other remained on the boat and poled through the rapids. As it was, we consumed about two hours in making the distance of about one mile. Here, after going through the inevitable police inspection, we were permitted to go ashore. My student went first to look up his cousin, Mr. Chen, who had been notified of our coming. In a short time he returned bringing Mr. Chen who greeted me in a most cordial manner, speaking in excellent English.

"We were immediately taken up to Mr. Chen's home and there I was treated to a wonderful drink of cold water, the first that was not boiling hot that I had tasted in four days. This had of course been boiled, but it was chilled before serving. As the afternoon was well advanced we only took a short stroll into the town and soon returned for a fine dinner of typically Chinese food, hence delicious. Afterward we sat out in the yard talking and giving the Kintehchen mosquitoes their evening meal. I was that night given a beautiful old Chinese bed, and thanks to a good mosquito net, had a very refreshing sleep."

After reading of Mr. Howe's trip from Nanchang to Ching-te-Chen, one can imagine the problems encountered by Marco Polo approximately 650 years before.

We arrive at our hotel, the Lotus Hall, at 5:15, exactly five hours after departing Nanchang. Waiting to greet us are Mr. Chang Sug-tao, Art Director of all of the porcelain factories as well as a member of the Friendship Association of the city, and Mr. Fang Chin-sen, of the Friendship Association. They assist us to our rooms and bid us goodnight. We are anxious to have a quiet dinner and an early evening.

The hotel rooms are modest and seemingly colorless. Perhaps it's because of the soot that permeates and coats everything in town, the result of coal mining and steel factories in the area. Grayness is everywhere and a sludge coats the hotel steps and sidewalks. There is, however, heat and hot water for an hour or two in the evening, the soap is quite good (smells like "Lifebuoy") and rooms are spacious.

Dinner is, as always, to our taste, almost a repeat of the excellent lunch. Mushrooms and chicken with hot red pepper, fish and mushrooms with garlic, vegetable soup, shredded pork and onions, rice, baked bread, a wonderful dark beer, mandarin

Lotus Hall, our hotel in Ching-te-Chen.

oranges and tea. All dishes are spicy, hot and sauteed in peanut oil.

Our first organized activity the next morning begins at 8:00 a.m. in a meeting room at the hotel. Mr. Chang and Mrs. Fang, over tea and cigarettes, give us our itinerary for our two-day visit and tell us some facts about Ching-te-Chen. We are anxious to compare current conditions with those reported by Père d'Entrecolles and Mr. Howe.

They state that the city's history goes back long before the birth of Christ. When we visit the museum, we'll see pottery from the area that dates to 4500 B.C. There are 230,000 people in Ching-te-Chen; another 200,000 in the suburbs. It is an isolated city that does most of its shipping by boat, just as in ancient times, although a railroad from Nanchang currently is under construction and is nearing completion. The Nan River goes through town and joins the larger Chang River on the outskirts. In the entire Kiangsi province there are 100,000 employed in porcelain factories, 25,000 of whom are in Ching-te-Chen. All clays are local or from within the province. Mr. Chang confirms that proto-porcelain was made here as far back as the birth of Christ and that white vitrified porcelain first was made in the Sui Dynasty (A.D. 589–618). Currently there are twenty factories producing porcelain. Most have been rebuilt since 1949, but on the same sites as the old ones. Kilns all are coal-fired.

Mr. Chang and Mr. Fang tell us that they don't ever recall Americans visiting Ching-te-Chen. If there were, it had to be prior to 1940. For fifteen years before the 1949 Revolution the factories here were closed. Because of the turmoil and upheaval caused by the war, there were no markets for their porcelains, no reasons to keep operating. The artists and craftsmen dispersed to other jobs, mainly to the farms. After the revolution the factories gradually were rebuilt and the old masters drifted back and began to rediscover their skills and train the young.

At 9:00 a.m. our briefing ends and we are off to see our first facility, the Wei Min Factory which means, "In the service of the people." Vice-Chairman of the Revolutionary Committee directing the factory is Mr. Chen Shu-chi. Wei Min began operating in 1958. We are told construction was done entirely by the workers. Its buildings cover 26,000 square meters and 2,000 people are in the employ. Main products are tablewares, tea and coffee sets and urns and vases of all sizes and shapes. In 1960 the factory produced 12,000,000 pieces of porcelain; in 1973, 30,000,000 pieces. Seventy percent is made for export.

As we are accustomed to doing, we have tea and cigarettes for about half an hour while Mr. Chen tells us about the factory and the workers. He recites the usual dogma of the teachings of Mao and the efforts of the workers who have brought about a "technical revolution through invention and innovation." He attributes 147 new suggestions and inventions solely to "the workers' dedication, hard work and determination for self-reliance." In particular Mr. Chen stresses how the company helps the worker throughout his lifetime. If a child is born, the worker is given extra pay to cover the costs of the nursery care. At age seven the child's schooling expenses are paid for. All through his education he is helped. Women retire at age fifty to fifty-five, men at age fifty-five to sixty, according to the job. A pension is given that can be as high as 90% of pay based on years of service. And the company eventually will pay for the worker's funeral.

When we tell Mr. Chen that in essence we do the same thing

through medical insurance programs, pensions, profit-sharing and life insurance, he seems impressed or surprised, we cannot decide which. It is doubtful that the virtues of our way of life have been much extolled to the Chinese.

Wei Min is largely geared to mass production similar to the factories of Tangshan. There is some hand decorating, but mostly transfer prints. The quality of the work is high. Kaolins of Ching-te-Chen are the world's best. Whiteness is as pure and as pristine as fine bone porcelain, enhanced by the carbon in the coal-fired kilns, and so strong and resilient is the clay that it supports itself down to eggshell thinness. Translucency is such that one feels he is looking at muted light bulbs in the hands of the artists and craftsmen at work. The maker's mark on the bottom of a small bowl or cup can easily be seen in detail through the porcelain.

In the materials preparation department eight large ball mills are mixing casting slip, and a machine turns out pug clay in a large roll with a diameter of about ten inches. The pug is of a putty-like consistency, fine grained and dense, smooth to the touch, and as hard as gelatin. It is sliced by hand with a wire tool into thin slabs, each to closely approximate the amount of clay needed to make a certain size bowl or platter. For cups, saucers and plates, smaller diameter rolls of pug are made. There are jiggers of all types, the most interesting of which is a double one that is semi-automatic. With the speed and coordination which comes from lots of experience, the craftsman alternately is throwing clay in two forms and pulling down the jiggers with both the left and right arms.

We see a number of innovative techniques in the glazing department. For coating the insides of cups there is a large tub of glaze with a simple foot pedal which, when depressed, sends up two small geysers of liquid glaze into two cups held upside down. The cups are exposed only for a split second, just to coat them thinly. In the West we generally use a spraying technique for this operation which takes longer and has the problems inherent in an air pressure system.

At the Wei Min Factory in Ching-te-Chen, eight large ball mills mix the casting slip, and a machine turns out pug clay in large rolls about ten inches in diameter.

Various glazing procedures were observed in Ching-te-Chen. *Above,* a young woman's hands work so quickly they are a blur. *Below,* a training session on the proper trimming of clay cups.

To glaze only the under surfaces of their shapes the Chinese rely on the hand and eye. As the bowls or saucers come by on a conveyor belt right side up, each is gripped in the center by a hand-held rubber suction cup. The craftsman then dips the bottom part of the clay piece into a tub of liquid glaze and quickly revolves it. The glaze is allowed only to come to the very edge of the piece; then the saucer is removed. Another split-second procedure.

For glazing only the tops of saucers and plates, a piece is centered deftly on a fast-spinning disc stationed in the center of another tub of glaze. A dab of glaze is applied to the center with a wide brush. The centrifugal force spreads the glaze suddenly and evenly and throws off the unwanted excess back into the tub.

The kiln room of Wei Min is about 500 feet long and houses the longest brick tunnel kiln we've seen, approximately 285 feet. Carts loaded with saggers bearing clay pieces slowly move on tracks into the beginning of the kiln while others bearing the fired porcelain exit from the far end, a never-ending procession. The firing cycle is twenty-four hours, the complete time it takes for a cart to go through the entire kiln. Heat at the midpoint of the tunnel builds up to 1290°C (2354°F), about the same as our level in Trenton (cone 10 down).

After inspection the pieces go into large rooms where transfer decorations of various kinds are applied. These are thin, transparent sheets which have color designs printed on them. Individual designs are cut from the sheets, dipped in water and applied to the correct location on a piece of porcelain. A damp sponge is used to smoothen and straighten the decalcomanias. When later fired, the paper will burn away and the color designs will knit indelibly with the glaze.

Kilns for color firings are smaller tunnel-types but are not automatic. Along the sides of the kilns are slightly elevated flat beds or roads about 24" wide with 2" high retaining walls on the outer sides. These roads are filled with pottery spheres about the size of a ping-pong ball which serve as large bearings or rollers to move the loaded racks of porcelain to the mouth of the kiln. It is an efficient and problem-free system. At the entrance to the kiln an operator turns a large metal screw clockwise to slowly move the load into the kiln, then unwinds to prepare for another rack.

Apparently word has spread about town that we are here. As we walk from the factory we are greeted with applause by a thousand or so curious people who have come to catch their first glimpse of Americans. Most are delightful children. In the best tradition of statesmanship Mrs. Boehm plunges into the crowd, gathers all the children around her, and poses for photos. It is interesting to see that, like people everywhere, the Chinese love to be photographed. Maurice and I notice several mothers pushing their youngsters up front and center to be certain they are included.

From Wei Min we are driven to the Ching-te-Chen Fine Arts Porcelain Factory. This is what we are eagerly waiting to see. This studio does only fine hand painting of tablewares, tea and coffee sets, vases and urns of all sizes, trays and porcelain paintings.

We are met by Mr. Sun Ching-pao, Vice Chairman of the factory and have tea and cigarettes while Mr. Sun tells us about the firm. He first carefully pays tribute to Chairman Mao and the workers and describes the rapid progress of the factory since it was re-established in 1954. "Innovation," "invention," "self-reliance," and "dedication" are all mentioned. We are not disturbed by the repetition of the party's credo and keep in mind that this exercise is not primarily for our benefit or edification, as the Chinese aren't so naive to think a great political impression is being made. Rather it is more a discipline and procedure practiced by the party leaders at every opportunity; sort of a pep talk and refresher course for all present.

We will see in this factory dozens of acerbic cartoons clotheslined at about a seven-foot height so all can read them. They are

The kiln for color firing, with its large metal screw and flat beds filled with pottery spheres that look like ping pong balls. *Below*, the teachings of Mao are prominently posted throughout the workrooms at Wei Min.

made by the workers and feature Lin Piao and Confucius in the most uncomplimentary ways.

The Fine Arts Factory employs 900. One hundred percent of what is produced here is for export. The work is too costly to be sold in the home market. It is used to help gain foreign currencies. The factory is only concerned with painting and firing of colors. The porcelains are completed to the white stage in another company, which we hope to see tomorrow, and sent over to the Fine Arts group ready for painting.

What we see in this studio will remain indelibly in our minds. These painters are the equal of the best in the world, and there are hundreds of them. The work is so fine that we mistakenly attribute some of it to decalcomanias; only later to be shown it is all by hand. Borders and shoulders of plates and saucers; rim and neck detail on urns and vases in hair-thin filigree; lacework and needlepoint designs: normally applied decalcomanias in Western work, here all are done by hand. Weeks and months are spent on individual pieces.

Handpainting is a highly developed skill at the Fine Arts Factory.

Most of the decorative designs are dominant, however, submerging the beautiful quality of the porcelain, and showing little of the restraint of the Yuan and early Ming periods. Decoration does not serve to complement the porcelain but seems rather to be an end in itself. Polychrome enamels ranging the spectrum of ceramic colors are used. The main source of design inspiration appears to be flowers, birds, butterflies, animals and fish, all repeated over and over again in painstaking detail. The virtuosity of the painter is emphasized, often at the expense of design taste.

It is apparent that this quality of work can only be done in a society where pay and costs have little relationship to the finished product. To produce the same in the West would not be possible because the costs and eventual pricing on each piece would be prohibitive. And tablewares and decorative objects simply do not command the price levels of porcelain paintings and sculpture. There is no question that with their excellent artistry and quality and low costs, the Chinese eventually could dominate the world markets in all of their handicrafts and arts, especially in fine porcelains.

One can only describe a few of the many outstanding pieces seen. A tall 30″ vase with a traditional shape commanded our attention. It is decorated in polychrome enamels with cherry blossoms and branches against a black background. Black is a difficult color to work with, as Mr. Boehm discovered in the first years of his studio. In the firing it consumes any color laid over or under it. To use other colors with black, the Germans developed a technique that starts with the application of black all over the object. With the use of tissue tracing paper, the design tediously is transferred onto the object using pin pricks to outline. The dry, unfired black color then is removed by picking it away from those areas in the design which are to receive other colors.

In 1951 Mr. Boehm and his artists completed 24 service plates and cups and saucers that have colorful flowers "dropped into" a black background. But the finished pieces had to carry such a high retail price they couldn't be sold. They are outstanding and among the most prized of Mr. Boehm's work.

The Chinese do the vase by painting the black by hand around the design areas which are later to receive the other enamels. Painting black by hand without leaving heavy brush strokes is difficult. In the West black and other solid ground colors are usually dusted, sprayed, or mixed into the slip.

The largest porcelain painting we see is a huge, romantic portrait of Chairman Mao as a young man of twenty-one. He is standing on a high hill, a book in his arm, sky behind, flowers at his feet, dressed in a full-length robe and with an ethereal, dream-like expression. The porcelain canvas is 60″ high by 40″ wide by approximately 1½″ thick. Style of the artistry is that of a Western-type, disciplined oil portrait. It is not at all Chinese in character.

Earlier I mentioned that such canvases pose problems as to standards of quality. These obviously are hand pressed from an open mold, as the thickness can vary as much as a quarter inch from side to side; and the surface is wavering. Like all others who attempt plaques, these artists experience severe firing problems. A few in work have noticeable warps and the glaze shows imperfections similar to those we saw in Tangshan.

The polychrome enamels sit high on the surface, not "into" the glaze as in our paintings. As explained in Chapter III, this is the nature of the once-fired glaze body. The greenware and the glaze knit together. We do an initial high firing on the greenware only. Then we cover the bisque porcelain with a lead glaze and put it through a second, lower firing. This keeps the glaze "on top of" the surface of the porcelain, a separate layer, so to speak, like icing on a cake. Our colors sink into the glaze in subsequent firings. The Chinese colors do not.

As a result, the Chinese need send their paintings through the decorating kilns once or, at most, twice. Our paintings receive up to eight different firings in order to sink the colors. In appearance the Chinese paintings seem very crisp, the detail and colors very "hard" with little of the softness, blend and diffusion we seek through multiple firings.

The Ching-te-Chen body, as described before, however, is unmatched for thin, delicate work because of its great strength and hardness. When fired the glaze completely permeates a thin wall inside and out giving a brilliant vitreous whiteness and magnificent translucency. This eggshell porcelain truly is "thin as paper, white as jade, bright like a mirror, sound like a bell."

Underglaze decoration still is an important part of the production in the Fine Arts Factory. It is produced in a building separate from the others. Here, too, the technique used is different from that generally used in the West. The artists paint their designs right on the fragile greenware, cradling the pieces between their knees on soft wool cushions. After completion of the painting, glaze is sprayed over the piece and it goes through its single high firing. In the West the procedure usually is to fire the greenware slightly to firm it up, after which the painting and glazing is done, followed by the high firing.

One of the most pleasing techniques still practiced is contrasting color. Underglaze blue and white is followed by overglaze decoration giving added depth and dimension and a pleasing contrast between the soft, diffused underglaze colors and the bright, crisp colors on top of the glaze.

Among the outstanding pieces in the exhibition room of the factory are two illuminated eggshell lamps in the shape of bowls. One is decorated entirely with butterflies, the other with fish in water. The porcelain is paper-thin and artists have painted the design on the inside as well as out. Butterflies and fish on the inner sides appear to be in the middle of the bowls.

All sizes and shapes of vases and urns are painted in this Fine Arts Factory. Two handmade planters are impressive. They measure about 32" in diameter and rise about the same height off the floor. The decoration on each is all by hand in miniscule detail. We are told it took a master artist approximately one year

Artists paint their designs right on the fragile greenware (underglaze painting), often cradling the pieces between their knees on soft wool cushions.

All sizes and shapes of vases and urns are hand-decorated in great detail in the Fine Arts Factory.

to paint the pair. Again, as with most pieces we see, the virtuosity of the painter results in supercharged all-covering decoration at the expense of the beautiful porcelain it has hidden.

If we are asked what, if any, substandard quality or techniques we see in the painting at the Fine Arts Factory, we would say in the application of gold. It is not of critical importance because it is not used to excess. And therein lies the problem. Because the emphasis is on economy and efficiency, pure gold is used sparingly. Most of the gold decoration is a thin bright gold that has a brassy appearance. It is particularly gaudy when used with cobalt colors. To our surprise, as in Tangshan, the acid-etch gold process is little understood and hardly used. What examples we see are primitive by fine English standards.

As we leave the Ching-te-Chen Fine Arts Porcelain Factory, located in the center of the city, we are greeted outside by a much larger crowd than at Wei Min. Just about everyone in town now knows of our presence. Again the pleasant, polite gesture of clapping, which we return. And again Mrs. Boehm gathers all the children around her for photographs. We are almost stampeded with friendship.

The three of us lunch alone at our hotel, as has become our custom. We've given up asking Mrs. Chang and Mr. Chou to join us. They will only do so for special luncheons or dinners given in our honor. The menu is pig's blood pudding with mushrooms and garlic, water buffalo tongue with leaks and water chestnuts, fish with bamboo, chicken with fungus and cabbage, vegetable soup, rice, bread, tea and mandarin oranges.

At 2:00 p.m. we leave to visit the Ching-te-Chen Porcelain Sculpture Factory. We all have high expectations, especially Maurice. Unfortunately, our expectations are too high. As with other factories we visited, the quality of the porcelain is high and the talents outstanding, but the emphasis is on production. Initiatives in efficiency, innovation and economy on the part of the craftsmen are actively encouraged, but freedom of expression in design and scale are therefore limited.

Furthermore, a good percentage of the sculptures are made for the home market and are used to carry Chairman Mao's political messages. Most of these are purchased by the government and placed in museums, schools, civic centers and other Chinese institutions. The figures generally are romanticized—handsome, muscular men; beautiful women; healthy, cherubic children. Subjects are military figures of both sexes, the "barefoot" nurses who carry medicine to the outlying provinces; peasants of all types performing all kinds of useful work, soldiers of the people, scenes from Tachai and Taching, etc. These are all meaningful to the Chinese.

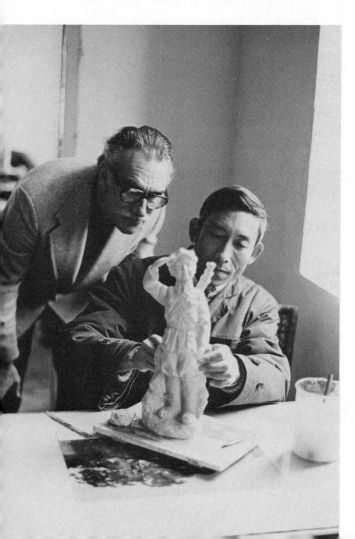

Political themes are often translated into porcelain. Here Maurice Eyeington observes the fashioning of a military figure.

The collection for export is of the character of any other extensive porcelain figurine line with emphasis on small scale, simply molded pieces. They are cast more heavily than the eggshell subjects of the Fine Arts Factory; and this is a different body. Less of the outstanding kaolins are used. It is not as white and the glaze is thicker.

Revolutionary Council Committee leader is Mr. Chu Whuntang. He explains that 600 are employed in the Porcelain Sculpture Factory. Selection of subjects numbers about the same but only about 100 are in production at one time. The factory began full operation in 1956. Presently about 1,000,000 pieces of sculpture a year are produced, an enormous quantity which, in itself, defines the quality level.

The fact that the potential for outstanding work is here is confirmed in the art rooms occupied by the senior sculptors. Although they spend most of their time on simple pieces, we see several models that compare with the finest work. A pair of peacocks (about 1/6 scale) with flowers has superb detail and finesse even though it is rococo in design. One young artist is working on a wonderful model of a young lady herding and training ten young deer leaping and running around her. This is the kind of work the West would particularly welcome. Too little of it is done.

Flower-making ability exists in the factory. A female designer is adding the finishing touches to a delicate spider chrysanthemum with foliage mounted on a celadon-colored plate. We are reminded of the quality of our Malvern studio's florals.

Another interesting piece in the making is a small ornate temple embodying extensive pierced and cutout work. This is a laborious and difficult technique of making lattice or grill walls by cutting with sharp tools fine designs through the unfired clay.

The volume of pieces further astounds us when we examine the production techniques. Very little slip casting is done. The most complex slip molds we see are comprised of four pieces; the majority are of two. And the molds are made with no locking

notches for precision; so the seams on the greenware pieces sometimes are pronounced.

Most of the models are produced from press molds. A pug
clay similar to that of the Wei Min factory is cut and shaped to
a size slightly larger than the open mold, then pressed by the top
half of the mold to form the sculptural image. Parts of models
are done this way, then joined together. Extensive tooling and
finishing follows.

Other models are produced by casting basic shapes out of
rough molds, then modeling in and adding the detail required.

Our system is more complicated. All our sculptures are slip
cast and mold work is extensive, the process perfected by German
studios. Beyond the first rough mold (waste mold) made from
an original clay sculpture, we do a second original model in
plaster of paris on which all fine details are carved. From this
refined plaster model we produce negative master (block) molds,
positive (case) molds and, finally, negative (working) molds for
our castings. Molds are precisely fitted and notched for proper
locking during casting.

Molds needed to cast parts of complex models can exceed 100
(151 for the "Birds of Peace"). The cast parts are assembled
piece by piece to build the model to its finished greenware structure. It is difficult to explain this process to our new friends.
There is a vast difference from two- and four-piece press molds
to slip casting with dozens of mold parts.

Coloring is done both by hand and by aerographing (spraying). One of, or a combination of, four different firing cycles
are used, depending on the piece and its colors: low, medium,
high and comprehensive. Most pieces go through a comprehensive kiln cycle at average temperatures over an average firing
time period.

We complete our visit to the figurine factory and still have
time to visit the local museum, the Ching-te-Chen Pottery and
Porcelain Hall. A disdain for the old is reflected in the imbalance of pieces in the collections. Only 500 represent the whole

More handiwork from Ching-te-Chen: Mrs. Boehm admires the delicate spider chrysanthemum mounted on a celadon-colored plate, and *below*, an artisan refines a clay relief design by hand-tooling.

of the glorious porcelain history of China prior to 1949; 2500 on display have been made since, many of which are politically oriented. This is correct according to Maoist and Marxist teachings. Although Mao has said, "We must not lop off our history," he also states, "Let the past serve the present." Yang Jung-Juo put it this way: "What we affirm is only that which has played a progressive role in history; as to things reactionary and conservative, we must firmly negate and criticize them."

The collections are heavily labeled for the benefit of the peasants. Displays are accompanied by detailed explanations and graphics that laud the workers and artists and disavow the contributions to art made during the past reigns of the emperors. Currently there are 1200 square meters of display area. This is being enlarged to 2,000 square meters. The institution also serves as an information center for the porcelain industry, providing research and reference materials. We are told that soon a cataloging of the collection will be compiled.

We arrive back at the hotel at about 5:30. It has been a long day, but it's not over yet. After dinner at 8:00 we are invited to watch some films, one of which is about Ching-te-Chen porcelains.

The films are interesting. The one on Ching-te-Chen is the shortest, only about twenty minutes. Another fascinating short piece shows closeups of Chairman Mao greeting guests as recently as the past October. The longest film (1½ hours) is all about the last "AAA" ping-pong tournament, "Little Silver Balls of Friendship," which involved dozens of national teams from Asia, Africa and South America. It was quite a spectacle of color, action and pageantry. Themes throughout are gratitude to Chairman Mao for his leadership and teachings, and friendship with foreign countries. The film lasts until 10:15.

Our schedule for December 9 is a tour of the Ching-te-Chen Research and Design Institute in the morning, lunch, a meeting from 2:00 to 4:30 attended by managers, designers and technicians, and a farewell dinner in our honor at 6:30.

The Institute is directed by Mr. Fang Ching, Vice Chairman. He is a pleasant, young, gracious man. Two hundred twenty-two are employed here, about half of whom are in a production facility connected to the Institute. Group responsibilities are creation of new designs and techniques, materials analysis, production studies, planning of new construction, technical services, and problem solving.

The technology is impressive and modern. We see spectrographic, chemical analysis and thermal equipment from the U.S., Germany, Japan and Switzerland. Laboratories are neat, clean and comfortably placed in house-like buildings. Trees and plantings provide an attractive outdoor setting.

All the techniques and processes of Ching-te-Chen porcelain-making are practiced and studied here, so we have an opportunity for a final close look at a cross-section of the industry. We are impressed with the direct, open answers given by Mr. Fang. We know there is an important difference between the thin, white body of the Fine Arts Division and the body used for figurines and household tablewares. Mr. Fang tells us it is the percentage of pure white kaolin used. Fifty percent is in the finest paste in combination with other clays, flint and feldspar. Only 30% is used in all other pastes.

The staff members of the Institute are, of course, professional and relaxed. We see outstanding work, including the sculptural area. Perhaps one day the industry leaders will slightly adjust their production emphasis and allow more concentration in the fine arts.

It is interesting to note that at one point one of us slipped and referred to tablewares as "china." No one understood what we meant, so we explained. All thought it very amusing. As we do at Boehm, they only use the word "porcelain" in describing their high-fired translucent ceramics. The term "china" is ambiguous but has continued in use in the West since the first shipments of porcelain from the Orient in the 15th and 16th centuries. Historically (in the West) it has been loosely applied to a variety of ceramic wares having little in common except that they are made of white-firing ingredients; and it continues in use to describe all kinds and qualities of ceramics. And when the nomenclature "bone china" is used, indicating the addition of calcined animal bone to the composition, it is equally misleading. It should be called "bone porcelain."

There was only one area of production we did not see even though we asked to: the making of the bowls, vases and urns in the eggshell thin, white body. We're not sure why as they've shown us just about everything else. Perhaps it was because at the Fine Arts Factory the day before we were told that all shapes were "thrown by hand," that is, made without the use of molds. We found this impossible to believe because of the extreme delicacy and thinness of the ware, the perfect symmetry of the shapes and the miniature pieces with squared-off shoulders and necks so small no finger could fit them.

Mr. Fang corrected the error and told us they were slip-cast; but perhaps they didn't want to pursue this. To show us they can throw by hand, he took us to a father and son who, with exceptional skill, were throwing quite thin (about $\frac{1}{4}''$) teapots and vases.

Paper thinness is achieved by taking a cast vase or bowl, revolving it on a disc and, with sharp tools, paring away unwanted clay until the ultimate in delicacy is achieved. It is this extraordinary skill we had hoped to see.

Through the morning at the Institute we have a great time. Good friendship and lots of laughs. The sculptors again talk Maurice into trying his hand with their modeling clays. As in Tangshan, the clays are different from ours, much softer. But they are able to see how Maurice approaches a new sculpture and handles the clay.

We return to the hotel from the Institute at about 11:30, so we have time to have lunch and to prepare for our 2:00 p.m. meeting. We've been driving through Ching-te-Chen for two days now and a picture of the small city and its people is emerging.

As mentioned, it is an isolated city and the people are provincial. It is like being in a small remote city in one of our sparsely populated states.

Ching-te-Chen is ancient and we do not see the great building activity of Tangshan and Peking. Homes generally are old and very modest. One could only describe many of them as hovels. Not all of the roads are paved. Only an occasional car is seen, some trucks and buses. Again we do not see a single horse or mule. Everything is moved by the people with hand carts. It is amazing to see the strength and determination of elderly men, women and children straining up and down the hilly streets of the city. Carts carry everything, including clays and porcelains, between factories. Men move from building to building at double-time speed while balancing a rack or board of delicate porcelains on one hand held above the shoulder.

As described by Père d'Entrecolles and Mr. Howe, the city is constructed with most streets running at right angles to each other; and some of the elegant old homes of the mandarins still exist. They presently serve administrative functions.

At the Ching-te-Chen Research and Design Institute we see extraordinary skill in hand-throwing and again enjoy a friendly exchange of ideas.

Industrial cities like Ching-te-Chen have severe pollution problems caused by energy and heat produced solely from coal. During our visit the fine silt is held down by a steady rain resulting in a gray-black mud everywhere.

From the nature of their homes and clothing, it does appear that the standard of living here is considerably lower than any we've seen so far, due to the isolation of the city. Tangshan, it will be recalled, is a major rail center with heavy commercial activity. Ching-te-Chen will begin to change dramatically once the new railroad network reaches it. The lives of the people will improve. Much of the mystery of the shrouded, protected city of porcelain will slowly evaporate.

Many of the personal habits and mannerisms of the Chinese are different from ours; or ours are different from theirs. They are especially vivid away from the larger, more cosmopolitan centers of population. Expectorating is widely practiced by both men and women of Ching-te-Chen. In our hotel spittoons are located about every twenty feet on both sides of the hallways. Bones are spit out on the tablecloth next to your plate. At meals burping is expected and soup is slurped loudly. Casseroles aren't passed; you simply stand up and reach across the table. We've finally discovered an advantage in the use of chopsticks.

The concern in China of a conflict with Russia is very real, as we see in Ching-te-Chen. The depth of this concern was clearly illustrated at the Wei Min Factory. Adjacent to the administration building a gaping hole was being dug deep into the ground. When asked what it was for we were told it will be a bomb shelter. Apparently the Chinese are building such shelters throughout the country.

Our 2:00 p.m. meeting is attended by about thirty people comprised of the Vice-Chairmen, designers and technicians from all the important factories. It started rather slowly, as all meetings do, so for once we took the initiative. These fine people had opened to us most of their precious techniques of making fine porcelain, which we did not think they would do. So we detail,

Tea and discussion in the afternoon. There were frequent meetings with artists and technicians.

as best we can, all our methods and practices.

During the exchange, Mrs. Boehm presents the porcelain panda to the group and a copy of our book. We also show them the last Bird of Peace plate we are keeping for presentation in Shanghai. The session really becomes lively. Technicians and artists fire questions at us and all exchanges are open and free. They are especially interested in the plate because it relates more to their work. Later Mrs. Chang discreetly tells us they would prefer to receive the plate rather than the panda, if it was all the same to us. So we switch the gifts. They complimented the Lenox glaze on the plate and expressed admiration for the gold acid-etch border.

The crowning gesture of friendship and trust comes when Mrs. Boehm suggests that they give us a pound or two of the fine pug clay to take back with us. We will make a cup and saucer from it, add gold acid-etch to the rim and border and return it to the Institute. They agree to do it. Traditionally, porcelain makers are loathe to release any information about their paste, let alone give a sample of it to be taken away. We value not only their generosity but also their trust.

Toward the end of the meeting they ask us to criticize their work, again using phrases like, "We want to learn from your experience;" "We must improve on what we are doing;" "We must learn from each other." This was like asking the student to criticize the teacher.

There isn't much to criticize, quite the contrary. We tell them their artists and craftsmen are the equal of the world's best; that their thin, white porcelain is the world's finest. There is nothing to compare with it. We assure them of our understanding that their current emphasis has to be on the mass-produced items both to try and meet the great needs of their people and to gain foreign currency. But we express the hope that one day more of their capacity will go toward the fine arts for this is what art collectors in our market and around the world would most appreciate.

The Chinese recognize their need for technology in the mass-produced porcelains. Even their decalcomanias apparently are made on simple equipment. They want to know all about decal printing machines in the West as well as any other equipment that might increase production.

We estimate that perhaps 350 million pieces of porcelain are produced in Ching-te-Chen and Tangshan combined. Including Foshan and other lesser areas, this might bring the total to 500 million a year; a tremendous amount. But not when you consider the average number of pieces used per person per meal (the Chinese use a lot of small dishes) which, conservatively, could be five per capita. If the population of 850 million held and no replacement porcelains were needed, it still would take about eight and one-half years of current production with no exports to satisfy their own tableware needs.

All Chinese exports are riding a wave of popularity in the present world markets, especially the arts and handicrafts. A good part of the appeal stems from a natural curiosity the world has to see and to have products not available for many years; and there is an emotional desire to reestablish understanding and communication through trade.

The boom should continue for a couple of years after which the novelty of Chinese goods will diminish and people will begin assessing their products as they would any others. At this point purchasing will become more selective and demand for the finest products will express itself. Hopefully the Chinese will respond to that demand and provide the world with more of the outstanding fine porcelains we've seen in Ching-te-Chen.

Our parting from all our new friends at the meeting is somewhat emotional. We have come to know and enjoy each other and all of us realize there is little chance we'll ever meet again. We'll take away fond memories and feelings for these gracious and talented people of Ching-te-Chen. We hope we've also left some.

In the evening a dinner party is given in our honor. Present with the three of us were Mrs. Chang, Mr. Chou, Mr. Chang, Mr. Ho, Mr. Fong and an important personage we hadn't met before, Mr. Li Ke-shih, head of the Friendship Association for the entire province of Kiangsi. Toasts to friendship and our two countries are frequent, about two per person, so we are on our feet often. All are made with the pungent mao tai or with rice wine.

The dinner is superb. There are fifteen or sixteen courses, depending on how you count them. And we eat some of each. Our hosts insist on it. Presentation is outstanding. Each course is a work of art. In one soup of sweet apples, the chef wrote "welcome friends" in egg whites. The complete dinner: chicken legs and thighs; preserved eggs (two years old) with cauliflower; tomatoes and peanuts; tripe with egg whites; sliced water buffalo beef; fried fish and potato chips; chili pepper; fried bean shoots; mushrooms stuffed with fish and tomatoes; fried steak cutlets; fish egg rolls; sweet apple soup with egg whites; chicken soup; fish soup; cabbage with bamboo and scallops; meat dumplings; thin apple pie; oranges; pears; bread; mao tai; rice wine; and tea.

At the conclusion of the dinner Mr. Li presents each of us with gifts of some of the precious porcelains of Ching-te-Chen. Mrs. Boehm presents the Bird of Peace plate and a book. We ask if, before we leave, we each may purchase a piece of the magnificent eggshell porcelain. Our request is generously approved. A bowl is purchased by Mrs. Boehm for about $130. We later will see a similar one in a Hong Kong shop for $1200. It is decorated in the *famille rose* palette, a symphony of birds and flowers in motion (see color plate).

We leave Ching-te-Chen at 8:30 the next morning, December 10, happy and high in spirits. We consider the visit a great success and we are proud to have been here. The feeling one comes away with is hard to describe. To be at the source and origin of something so important is a fulfilling and humbling experience. Ching-te-Chen is synonymous with porcelain. Here it seems a part of life just as getting up in the morning is. Many of these people have done little else through generations of their families.

About two hours into the return trip, Mr. Ho, our expressive friend, suddenly starts gesticulating excitedly and appears very upset. Mrs. Chang explains that he is angry with himself because he forgot the lump of fine clay that was promised to us. Mrs. Boehm calms him in her understanding way and suggests that perhaps if someone is traveling from Ching-te-Chen before we depart China, they may be able to place the sample on a flight from Nanchang to Canton where we will spend the last two days of our trip. We doubt that we will receive the clay.

The return drive from Ching-te-Chen back to Nanchang is especially grueling. It rained heavily all night and continues to rain this morning. The dirt and clay roads are difficult to maneuver. On one muddy hill the tires sink so deep the under-carriage is almost torn out.

We again stop at the halfway point in the same country hotel, this time for lunch. It is very cold and there is no heat. Rain has partially turned to sleet. The kind landlord fills a metal tray the shape of a wok with charcoal and starts a fire. It's not enough to warm the room but we are able periodically to thaw out our frozen feet and fingers. In spite of the discomfort we eat an excellent lunch of turtle soup (shells and all, just caught in the back pond), poached mandarin fish (a delicate white fish that tastes like trout, the best we've had yet) with pork and fungus, cabbage soup with chestnuts, bread, rice, beer and oranges.

We reach Nanchang Airport at 3:30 p.m., seven hours after leaving Ching-te-Chen. The overcast is heavy and we are told our plane will be at least an hour late. Departure for Shanghai had been scheduled for 4:30. We'll leave between 5:30 and 6:00. Mr. Ho orders another tray with charcoal and we are quite comfortable as we wait for our plane.

CHAPTER XI

Shanghai

THE FLIGHT from Nanchang to Shanghai takes three and one-half hours because of a one-hour stop in Hangchow. Arrival in Shanghai is at 9:00, twelve and one-half hours after leaving Ching-te-Chen. We are met by Mr. Shang Juo-chien, Mrs. Yung Yu, and two younger members of the Association. Our accommodations are at the "Peace Hotel," an elegant fifty-year-old structure obviously built by a Western family. (It is believed that Noel Coward wrote *Private Lives* here.) It is large and comfortable with good plumbing and heating and hot water all day long. Most of the staff speak English. There is an extensive Western menu for those who are homesick or nonadventurous. Once again the odd couple, Maurice and I, have to share the same room.

We want to go straight to bed but our new hosts insist that we at least have a snack. Mrs. Boehm tries to excuse us, telling all in detail about how tired we are and how hungry we are not. At the end of her presentation she says "Do you mind if we miss dinner?" Whereupon one of our new hosts replies in a friendly manner, "Yes, we do." So we have a snack and finally get to bed about 11:00. No one will starve in China!

Because we have laundry to send out, are tired and a bit sick (Mrs. Boehm and I both now have colds), our new hosts permit us to start our program for December 11 at 10:00 a.m. We meet in Mrs. Boehm's room after a good breakfast. Mr. Sen is not present so Mrs. Yung takes over with the help of her two young assistants, Miss Tchai and Mr. Wong.

The Chinese always have your itinerary planned in detail, but as a courtesy they first will ask you what you would like to see and where you would like to go, fully realizing you probably don't know enough about anything to make a sensible suggestion. Our polite reply, as usual, is that we will rely fully on their good suggestions for the duration of our visit. Mrs. Yung then goes through the program step by step, pausing at each point to get our approval. This procedure takes about thirty minutes.

The remainder of the morning is spent visiting the Shanghai Industrial Equipment Exhibition held in a huge hall quite near our hotel. On display are large and small generators, tool and die machines, laser and other kinds of cutting and drilling equipment, scale models of engines for ships, farm machines, huge presses, telecommunications equipment, cars and trucks.

In the light industries' section we see displays of all the arts and handicrafts, cooking utensils, clothing and fabrics, sporting equipment, some medical equipment, candy, dental items, plastics and other items for the home. The most impressive sight is a chunk of carved jade, uniformly green in color, with forty-one mountain climbers in various postures and positions. The carving weighs two tons, having come from a stone of three tons. It looks like a small mountain of jade. The Revolutionary Council leader of the jade factory later tells us it took twelve men six months to complete the carving. It is priceless.

We return for lunch at 12:30. The menu is egg and spinach soup with fungus, sweet and sour pork with bamboo, chicken with bamboo and sweet leeks, fish and sweet leeks, fried bean sprouts, rice, toast, beer, coffee and oranges.

At 2:00 we leave to visit two handicraft factories which happen to be adjacent to each other, Peking Jade and Ivory Carving Factory, and Shanghai Carpet and Tapestry Factory. The carving factory is similar to what we saw in Peking, only much larger and more specialized. Seven hundred ten carvers and polishers are working on jade, ivory, quartz, malachite, lapis, onyx and other semi-precious stones. Most of the raw stones come from the southwestern provinces, some from Tanzania. The ivory also comes from southwest China.

Above the Shanghai Industrial Equipment Exhibition, a large
inscription urges greater mechanization to help build socialism.

Weavers at the Shanghai Carpet and Tapestry Factory working on a 30-foot
tapestry of the Great Wall destined for the UN Building in New York.

Eighty percent of the carvings are exported. The same is true of the handwoven carpets and tapestries which also are from a big factory of 800 weavers and designers. All pieces are made from woolen and cotton fabrics. In stock are 700 different color dyes. In some tapestries as many as 300 may be used. Subject matter covers five categories: Peking (traditional, old designs), florals, antiques, historical, and natural (environmental). The average weave used is ninety woven strands per square inch. A good percentage of the finished carpets seem to be sculptured. This factory represents the fourteenth fine art and handicraft we've seen in China.

We return to the Peace Hotel at 4:30. Our hosts inform us they've planned entertainment for the evening. The Shanghai Acrobatic Troupe, the same group which performed for former President Nixon, is in town. In fact we'll be in the same seats he and his party occupied. We are to leave at 6:45 after dinner.

Shanghai cuisine, subtle in its seasoning, impresses us. But we've thoroughly enjoyed all the cooking we've experienced to date. For dinner we have fried spinach, egg and fungus soup, fish with sweet leeks, pork with bamboo and mushrooms, fried beef cutlets, rice, bananas, oranges and coffee.

The acrobatic performance is outstanding, one of the best we've seen. Our seats are in the center at floor level. The arena is attractive and comfortable and holds about 2,000. All seats are filled. We notice a few Westerners near us.

Audiences here are very quiet. During and after each act our impulse is to clap loudly, sometimes cheer. Usually we are all alone in our enthusiastic plaudits, although some Chinese seem to be joining us as the night progresses. The show moves along quickly with short introductions and with none of the hoopla and buildup given Western circus-type performers. We see and enjoy a lot in two hours, and then head back to the hotel.

This morning, December 12, our colds have fully blossomed, but we're determined to maintain the schedule. Mercifully our hosts cancel the trip to a commune in the suburbs as the weather is poor and they can see we are under it. Instead we spend the morning inside at the Shanghai Friendship Store where we buy more gifts. It is interesting to note that we've not yet seen any of the fine art porcelains of Ching-te-Chen in any store. Apparently all that are made are subscribed to in advance and find their way to selected foreign markets. The United States is not among them.

We return to the hotel at 11:00 a.m. so we may have an additional hour of rest before our afternoon schedule. It is welcome. Our lunch is cabbage and chicken soup, prawns with sweet and sour sauce, pork meat balls, fried chicken with shredded pepper and carrots, green cabbage, steamed dough, rice, beer and coffee.

In the afternoon we have a wonderful time at one of Shanghai's Children's Palaces. As mentioned before, youngsters leave the nurseries at age seven and begin middle school. Organized study lasts from 8:00 a.m. to 3:00 p.m. When school is out, all middle school children (seven to fourteen years of age) attend a Children's Palace from 3:30 to 5:30. There are ten in the city of Shanghai.

The Palaces provide a place for recreation and additional study and practice in the arts and in vocational areas. We are told the children are encouraged in the directions of their personal interests. In large part this appears to be on-the-job training for eventual career work. The high levels of skill we see indicate that many of the students spend most of their daily Palace time hard at work at their chosen art or vocation. We see advanced skills in needlework, auto mechanics, music, ballet, painting and drawing, singing and conducting, closed circuitry, model ship building, electrical equipment, model airplane construction, etc. When their schooling has been completed, this new generation will be prepared to make immediate contributions to their society.

The Palace we visit has 800 children and forty instructors. We are greeted by the Revolutionary Council leader of the school, a woman, and four youngsters of varying ages who obviously were selected because of their brightness and warm personalities.

At the Children's Palace, the studious mien of these older musicians contrasts with the more lighthearted spontaneity of the younger ones.

From their comments and actions, it is apparent these youngsters have done this before. They are gracious and friendly, always taking us by the hand, and address us as "auntie" and "uncle."

We really have a lot of fun. The first game we try is throwing bean bags with a shovel in an attempt to hit a furnace opening. Mrs. Boehm takes a ride on a large rocking horse. We try our skill at knocking down a cardboard figure of Confucius with bows and arrows. And, of course, we engage in ping-pong with the children and are soundly trounced.

We then are taken to a series of performances staged for our pleasure. Eight very young people in gay costumes enact a story with dance and song. Two different age groups play selections on instruments that approximate mandolins. Another group is all accordians, another all violins, and there is a full orchestra with all instruments. A large chorus awaits us on another floor. Around and around we go through the huge building enjoying the amazing skills of these intensely trained children.

Each selection presented deals with political themes of the "new China." Even the song and dance by the youngest tell of little Red Guards helping in the oil fields. Tachai and Taching are main themes. Chairman Mao and his teachings of "self-reliance," "taking from the past only what is useful to serve the present," "building together," "serving the people," etc., are often mentioned, as are the enemies of the people, imperialists, and followers of Confucius and Lin Piao.

Chinese society is child-conscious. As Mr. Chou said, "It is important that children learn to serve the people and the state. We give our full attentions to the proper development of our children. They are China's greatest asset." And they are treated as such. The adults consider the children a privileged class, consciously giving them a sense of love and caring. They emphasize modesty, group acceptance, friendship, cooperation, unselfishness and the submergence of self. Chairman Mao teaches that these qualities in the young are essential to maintaining a sound classless society with future generations.

Discipline is thorough but is not accomplished by threat or force. Rather it is done by repetition of political themes. Art, music, books, teachers, model students, radios, newspapers, bulletin boards and the large red signs around the city all carry the same messages. If you ask one of the youngsters what he or she wants to do when grown up, you receive an answer such as, "I will work in the fields to help our people and to further the aims of our socialist motherland." The tenets of Chairman Mao are learned thoroughly and a huge cadre of young party members is everywhere to see they are not forgotten.

The system seems to work for the Chinese. There appears to be intense motivation to excel, for improving one's efficiency and productivity for the people, not for personal gain. The self *is* submerged in the interest of the state. The result is a system with clearly defined divisions of labor and activity. This huge labor-oriented society mobilizes and directs its masses.

Much attention at the Children's Palace seems to be given to friendship and peace with all people of the world. Each of the groups of children warmly applaud us as we enter and depart their rooms; and in unison they repeat, "Welcome our American aunty and uncles," and "Goodbye to our American aunty and uncles."

Finally there is a sense of pride and self-confidence in the children, from the very youngest. They seem not to be shy nor inhibited. Any of them will shake hands, look you in the eye and answer your questions in a loud, clear voice.

Yet we wonder about the individual identities of these children. What are they really like? The children almost seem programmed, like automatons. It is in the older children that one sees the effects of uniformity the most. While performing many appear expressionless, unemotional. They almost seem to be disconnected from their activities. Yet in the very young, who haven't been exposed to the teachings for long, there remains some individual charm and natural, spontaneous expression.

One can only hope that the system will allow some individuals to pursue their interests and aptitudes. If not, the intellectual and creative processes in China will move forward at a snail's pace.

Before departing the Children's Palace we have tea and exchange gifts. Mrs. Boehm presents the porcelain sculpture of the young Giant Panda Cub to the leader and children. The youngsters present each of us with examples of their handicrafts and art. We say goodbye to our little friends. Mrs. Boehm hugs each of them warmly.

The farewell dinner given in our honor by the Shanghai Branch of the Chinese People's Association for Friendship with Foreign Countries is held in a private room at the Peace Hotel. Present are our constant companions and the four members of the local association. Like Peking and Ching-te-Chen, the dinner is outstanding in quantity, quality and presentation.

The menu: Appetizers of ham, eggs, tomato, fungus, sweet leeks, pork, squid, gizzard (duck), eggroll, prawns, fried jellyfish and peanuts. Main courses of shrimp with bamboo shoots, fried duck with pineapple, meat dumplings, sesame and rice

A parting gift of the Giant Panda Cub to our friends at the Children's Palace.

dumplings in a sweet soup, crabmeat with cabbage, mandarin fish with chestnuts and mushrooms, pork meat balls, a potpourri stew, steamed dough, rice, oranges, apples, mao tai, sweet wine, beer and tea.

We arise early this morning, December 13. Our short stay in Shanghai is over. We must be on our way to Canton. We haven't had an opportunity to see much of Shanghai in our two days, but we've formed a few strong impressions.

We are certain that Shanghai is one of the noisiest cities in the world. The Peace Hotel is close to the Huang Poo River, a busy waterway with ships of all sizes and types which blow their loud horns as they approach the city. This is added to the horn-happy auto, truck and bus drivers. And to complete the cacophony, a large bell across from our hotel peels on the hour around the clock.

The city is different from Peking. As a port city it is more cosmopolitan, and the people seem more relaxed. As the center of government with wide streets and spanking new buildings, Peking has a rigid atmosphere. Everyone seems to be at attention, and the streets are empty by 9:00 p.m. Not so in Shanghai.

This city is the largest in population in China, with about twelve million. It sprawls over a wide area like Los Angeles. There are thousands of small shops and a few very large department stores; all seem to have a lot of activity.

Shanghai is China's largest commercial and industrial center. Everywhere we've been we've seen its products, including most of the cars, beers, wines and cigarettes. We all wished we had more time to enjoy this interesting city.

Our Friendship Association hosts accompany us to the airport for our flight at 1:30 p.m. We are overwhelmed when, just as we are to board the plane, one of the staff from the Peace Hotel comes running with two wooden clothes hangers I had left and a pair of sheer stockings which Mrs. Boehm had knotted and thrown away because of severe runs. He drove sixteen miles to return our property to us. The stockings were clean and neatly pressed!

CHAPTER XII

Huangchou (Canton) and Foshan's Ceramics

As WITH ALL of our flights in China, our trip to Canton is comfortable, this time on another new British Trident. We cover the 900 or so miles in less than two hours. Our new hosts awaiting our arrival, Mr. Chen Chou-li, one of the chief members of the Friendship Association, and Professor Kao Yung-jain, from the ceramic art department of Canton University. Mr. Chen speaks English. Both will accompany us on our trip to Foshan. Professor Kao originally was with the Foshan ceramic industry from which he was transferred to the University a few years ago.

The Friendship Association here has a large staff which is kept busy the year round, especially during the Fairs when 25,000 foreign traders come to town. For the first time people almost ignore us. They've seen quite a few Americans and other Westerners here.

Canton is a 2400-year-old subtropical city of 3,000,000 people whose primary functions revolve around world trade. Through the Fairs it conducts about half of China's annual trading. The rest is handled directly with Peking, some through Shanghai, by the State trading corporations.

In addition to being the trading city, Canton serves other purposes. It is a showplace of socialist achievement; sells Chinese products to earn foreign exchange; centralizes business; and gathers intelligence about world pricing, products, marketing, packaging, etc.

137

Not stock averages, but a table of the several ingredients of Chinese porcelain showing the slight variation through the years from the Ming Dynasty's classic formula, shown in the last column.

早期瓷器和明代瓷器胎质成份及烧成温度比较表

化学成份	郑州二里岗 商代早期瓷器	陕西张家坡 西周早期瓷器	安徽屯溪 西周早期瓷器	山西侯马 战国早期瓷器	江西 万历
硅 酸 (SiO₂)	76.38%	75.46%	71.95%	78.81%	71
氧化铝 (Al₂O₃)	14.91%	17.55%	19.28%	14.15%	20
氧化钾 (K₂O)	2.06%	2.75%	3.24%	1.36%	3
氧化钠 (Na₂O)	0.79%	0.23%	0.57%	0.55%	1
氧化铁 (Fe₂O₃)	2.27%	1.48%	1.83%	1.97%	1
氧化钛 (TiO₂)	0.91%	1.13%	1.11%	1.25%	0
氧化钙 (CaO)	0.67%	0.41%	1.48%	1.00%	1
氧化镁 (MgO)	1.18%	0.95%	0.51%	1.13%	0
氧化锰 (MnO)	0.09%	0.03%	0.03%	0.04%	0
烧成温度	1200±20℃	1200±20℃	1230±20℃	1230±20℃	123

早期瓷器在胎质成份经成火度上是和明代景德镇的瓷器基本近似的

Chinese curios in Canton: a drainpipe, artfully embellished and made entirely of porcelain, and a canopied bed.

We stay at the Canton Guest Hotel located in the heart of the city away from the Fair complex. The structure reminds us of a southern plantation set several hundred yards behind beautiful flowering gardens. It is a magnificent building erected by Western interests years ago. The rooms are huge, the beds firm and surrounded completely by sheer mosquito netting falling from a round canopy. Now the building is practically empty with just a few other guests besides ourselves. Our hosts tell us that the Guest Hotel serves to accommodate only foreign dignitaries and friends of China.

The rest of our luggage is waiting here for us. We are startled when we see how much we've accumulated. We started the trip with four large cases. We now have ten.

We are given fifteen minutes to freshen up. Our hosts want us to see an extensive traveling exhibition of Foshan ceramics at the local museum. They held the show over one day for us. Tonight it will be packed and sent on to Peking. It is late in the day so we are able only to have a cursory look at the collection. The pieces are distinctive, different from sculpture we've seen anywhere. This is due to the different clays, which have a natural color ranging from brown to light tan and white, and the technique of glazing only the bases, flora, and the garments on the figures.

Arms and faces of human figures and most animals are left in a natural, unglazed state similar to ours. The ceramic bodies are not porcelain. They are fine-grained, durable, highly-fired stoneware similar to Wedgewood's jaspar and basalt wares; and there are earthenwares. Foshan has been producing stoneware and pottery for over 700 years.

On the way back to the hotel our new hosts tell us they are giving a dinner in our honor this evening. We have one hour to collect ourselves and to try to find a second wind.

Joining our inseparable fivesome are four members of the Friendship Association, including Mr. Chen and Professor Kao. Once again we share repeated expressions of friendship through

Expressions of friendship are always on the menu when we dine with our Chinese hosts.

toasting. It is fun tonight taking our turns at "campei" (down the hatch) with wine rather than mao tai!

We had been told we would most enjoy Cantonese food because it is sweeter and more like Chinese-American cooking. The dinner is elegant and excellent in all respects. After appetizers of peanuts, sliced egg and vegetable omlet, sliced dried liver, hot pepper garnish, carrots and bamboo, fried jellyfish and pickled turnips, we proceed to main courses of frogs legs with broccoli; spring rolls (egg rolls); whole turtle soup with fungus; squid with mushrooms; kidney and cabbage, whole carp with roe; leeks and mushrooms; glutinous rice cakes with sesame; egg cake with coconut filling; oranges; tangerines; fried rice with ham, egg and green pepper; and tea.

We are in bed by 10:00 and looking forward to our next full day in Foshan.

At 6:30 the morning of the 14th, we are awakened from sound sleep and are greeted by unusually cool weather. It has dropped to 48° in our rooms, and is colder outside. It should be in the 70s.

The weather changes often and dramatically here. Mr. Chen, Professor Kao and an English-speaking associate, Tan Chin-Lung, accompany us to Foshan. The trip by car takes one and one-half hours. Even in winter the countryside of Kuangchou Province is beautiful. Small communes with winter wheat and rice fields border the road. They repeat themselves north all the way to the Yangtze River. Water is everywhere on this delta. The Pearl River spreads into four main tributaries with dozens of lesser ones. But the hazards of road travel are no less difficult here. All over China the people vie with each other for road space.

Our first stop in Foshan is a large building which serves as a reception center for the city. Because of its proximity to Canton, Foshan receives many foreign guests, so the art of hospitality and welcome are frequently practiced here. Waiting to greet us are Hsu Ching-chi, Revolutionary Council leader of the Foshan welcoming committee, Yang Kuo-chiu, Revolutionary Council leader of the Fine Arts Factory, and several associates. We stay only for introductions, then re-enter our cars to spend the rest of the morning viewing an ancient temple.

Initially we aren't overly enthusiastic about this. Again it is rainy and cold and we have seen many temples during our two brief weeks in China. But we are pleasantly surprised. The Foshan temple is perhaps the most beautiful we've seen, although it is difficult to make such comparisons. It is large, segmented into lavish rooms and courtyards, and almost every square foot seems to be encrusted with ceramic sculpture, painted lacquer figures, and gilded bronzes and wood carvings.

It is a Sung Dynasty structure, built about 880 years ago, rebuilt a couple of times during the Ming and Ching periods. The most unforgettable feature is a $2\frac{1}{2}$-ton Taoist Buddha of bronze with enamel over-coloring. The casting is superb. It is an outstanding example of the great bronzes for which China is so renowned.

The director of the museum gives us a host of other facts about the temple and Foshan. Part of his presentation, of course, is about the past and present uses of the temple and how it now fits into Chairman Mao's teachings. "Prior to liberation," he said, "the reactionary ruling classes used it for religious activities in order to bully the people. Now, according to Chairman Mao, we must let the past serve the present. The temple serves to expose cheating of the reactionaries and reminds the people of the past evils. Our people are the masters who created this temple and now they use it as their own."

Foshan has a recorded history of nearly 1300 years, back to the early Tang Dynasty. It always has been one of the famous towns of China. In fact, Foshan and Ching-te-Chen were two of the four most famous towns all during the Sung Dynasty. The city boasts of a wider range of arts than Ching-te-Chen, however. In addition to ceramics, Foshan is known for its silks, outstanding bronze sculptures and castings, wood carving, paper cutouts, and a host of other paper, bone, wood, wax and stone decorative subjects. Population is 160,000 in the city; 230,000 including the suburbs. The fourteen ceramic factories employ 20,000 workers. Eight thousand are in art and decorative ceramics. The Fine Art Factory employs 530. Exports are about 60% and reach five continents.

After leaving the temple we return to the reception building for lunch. We have soup with pork meat balls, leeks, tomato and cabbage; appetizers of dried pork, peanuts, pig's hooves, onions, chili peppers, carrots and turnips; main courses of fried chicken with puffed prawns, fried fish fillets, sweet and sour pork, chicken with mushrooms and cabbage, beef with tomato and bamboo, omelette with leeks, whole carp with mushrooms and water chestnuts, steamed rice, wine, beer, oranges, tangerines and tea.

We comment that the soup here is served first. Mr. Hsu says they do it for our sake because it is done so in America. Unlike Chinese-American restaurants where the soup, rice and fish courses usually are served first, in China they generally are served last, just before sweets.

At about 1:30 we are on our way to the Foshan Shih Wan Art

Porcelain and Pottery Factory. Shih Wan is the ceramic district located on the outskirts of the city. From what we saw at the exhibition last night, we know that this is the outstanding figurine factory in China.

What puzzles us in the use of the word porcelain to describe their high-fired body. We don't question it, but by Western definitions it is an opaque stoneware. Clays of different colors are decorated in the greenware stage with thick color glazes, then fired once at high temperatures. We are told that white pieces are fired as high as 1300° C (2372° F), about the same temperature of high-fired porcelain; but little of the translucent-giving feldspar is used.

Earthenware pieces, also of varying colors, go through two firings. The first is the unglazed body firing at about 1050° C (1922° F), a temperature approaching normal stoneware levels. After decoration with color glazes the pieces go into the decorating kiln with temperatures between 700 and 900° C (1292 to 1652° F).

Production emphasis is on sculptures of people and animals, with some tablewares and miniature figurines (referred to as "toys" by our hosts). A remarkable total of about 1,000,000 pieces will be made in this one factory this year, most, of course, of the simple two-piece mold variety. Of 3000 different subjects, about 300 are in production at one time. Thirty different color glazes are used. All clays are locally mined. About 70% of the staff of 530 are women. (More men work in the heavier, industrial ceramic factories.)

After tea and a close look at the extensive collection in the exhibition rooms, Mr. Yeng conducts us on a tour of the factory. We are hoping he will take us to every part of the operation, especially the modeling and moldmaking departments. We haven't seen moldmaking the entire trip.

We are not disappointed. Our first stop is modeling and moldmaking for stoneware figurines. At first we are surprised to see only females in the mold department. In our studios it is strictly a male function. On investigation we understand why. As described before, our process involves extensive molding starting from the clay model through waste molds, plaster model, master molds, case molds and working molds. These many steps are necessary in order to transfer the precise finished detail from the sculptured plaster model into the working molds from which cast parts are taken. The molds are many and heavy and must be handled by our men.

The Chinese make fewer and simpler molds, and directly from the original clay model. No refined plaster model is made and only the rough basic structure or form is molded. The casts, of course, are similarly "unfinished." These are entirely re-tooled by hand and all small parts and accouterments are made from clay by the artisans.

Stoneware and pottery clay slip are very thick with a viscosity similar to molasses. They quickly "set up" in the molds and can be removed within a few minutes. The thickly-cast clay is malleable and plastic, very unlike fragile porcelain-making clays;

At right and on page 145, workers
make mold parts from clay model parts
at the Foshan Shih Wan
Art Porcelain and Pottery Factory.

About one million sculptures, mostly of people and animals, are produced a year here. "Unfinished" casts are entirely retooled by hand and small parts are made from clay by the artisans.

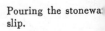
Pouring the stonewa[re] slip.

Removing the casting.

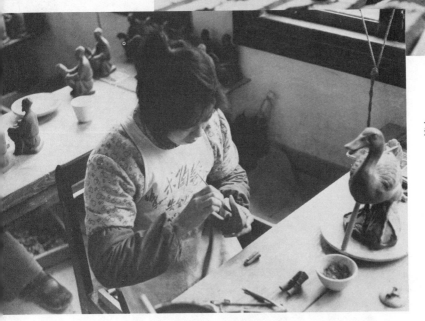

Assembling and fini[sh] ing the greenware.

Putting the finishing touches to the assembled greenware models.

Over a work area, signs encourage dedication to work to achieve "supreme results."

The sculpting of the clay model, where it all begins.

so mold parts can be separated with little concern for the unfinished castings. Also, because of these characteristics, quite complicated castings can be made from a single mold. We separate one complex mold and count the interlocking plaster sections. There are thirty-nine! Our most complex molds usually don't exceed two dozen parts.

Techniques of moldmaking and materials used, however, are exactly the same as ours. It is interesting to see the artisans sectioning off various parts of a model and the manner in which they prepare and pour the thickening plaster-of-paris. We are anxious to show our male moldmakers photographs of their Shih Wan female counterparts.

Artisans in the greenware assembling and finishing department work as we do. First they take the rough cast parts and trim away mold seams and rough spots. Using a gelatinous-like slurry of clay, they join the parts together. Fine parts are made up by hand and added to the developing model. The final step is tooling. Texture of clothing, character of faces and hands, hair or fur on animals, feathers of birds, veining of leaves, etc. all are added with the use of modeling tools.

Clays of different colors may be combined on a single model. A white cape or hat is made from the white clay so no later coloring is needed. Brown leather parts or tools similarly are made from brown clay; and so on.

The completed stoneware models go into the decorating department in the unfired greenware state. Unlike the Ching-te-Chen underglaze work where the artists have to handle carefully the thin fragile clay, the Shih Wan dried clay is heavy and less care is needed. Thick color glazes are applied by brush. For detail of faces and other unglazed parts, colors similar to ours are used.

There are two large kiln complexes at the Fine Arts Company. One is a tunnel kiln. The other is most unusual and can only be described as a series of "cave" kilns which first were constructed during the Sung Dynasty (A.D. 960–1280). A long building stretches vertically against the side of a hill which has about a

Cave kilns, first constructed during the Sung Dynasty, are still in use.

30° pitch. On the left side of the building is a series of steps and landings leading to the top. To the right is the unbroken original surface of the hill into which caves have been cut at different levels. The caves are lined with refractory bricks. Down the slope below each is a furnace for firing. Most of the large earthenware vases and urns are fired in these cave kilns.

One might wonder about the retention of sensitive colors such as reds, oranges and pinks in the high heat of the once-fired stoneware kilns (1300° C). On our porcelain body these colors can take temperatures of only 750 to 800° C and the temperature control is critical. Two much heat burns them away.

The difference is this. Our painting is applied to a once or twice-fired body. Colors are thinly applied and rest on a hard, impervious surface. The unfired stoneware clay body has great absorption and the colors deeply penetrate. In addition the colors are in the form of thick glazes. Some of the color may burn away in the intense heat but most of it melds and fuses with the body.

After our tour we return to the meeting room for more tea and discussion. The session is similar to those in Tangshan and Ching-te-Chen but not as thorough in Shih Wan because of the brevity of our visit. Gifts are exchanged. Mrs. Boehm presents to the Factory our remaining Panda sculpture. (We had carried the Pekin Robin sculpture and the Pandas all the way from Trenton without any mishaps!) In behalf of the Shih Wan potters, Mr. Yang presents each of us with a fine stoneware sculpture from the Fine Arts Company.

During the meeting Mrs. Boehm invites the group to propose an appropriate name for the Panda sculpture. This stimulated a great deal of discussion and fun. It was a repeat of what had been done at the Children's Palace where she received two suggestions, "Yu Yi" meaning "friendship," and "Yu Hao" meaning "friendly." Our Shih Wan friends finally agreed on "Dong Dong" which translates to "winter, winter." Our choice is "Hsuehling" ("Shur-ling") which means "snow bear."

Our drive back to Foshan is slowed by late afternoon traffic. It affords the last opportunity we have for conversations with our hosts in our separate cars. Talk is, as usual, freely exchanged. Although they strongly espouse their system and way of life, our Chinese friends allow us to speak of America with equal pride and intensity.

Two main points of interest concerned Taiwan and Hong Kong. The Chinese always include Taiwan as one of the twenty-nine provinces of the People's Republic of China. They are unequivocal in claiming it and are sure it's just a matter of time before it again comes under their control. When asked how this would be accomplished the reply was "reclaiming the island, which is rightfully ours, warrants any action that is necessary."

Hong Kong is similarly regarded. They speak of it as theirs and express the opinion that one day the British will have to "give it back." They dislike the proximity of this booming city with its "attractions of the flesh and Western luxury." Prostitution, black-marketing and gambling always are mentioned in speaking of

Hong Kong. The Chinese would like to "clean it up and remove the capitalists." The commercial value of the city to the P.R.C. is not mentioned.

After our long and outstanding lunch we are not hungry and settle for a light dinner with beer. We have a lot of packing to do tonight. We've decided to rearrange our bags in hopes of checking the bulk of them at the airports in Hong Kong and Tokyo.

As we enter our rooms we hear Mrs. Boehm howl with laughter. We rush to investigate. The night before she had requested a bed board, and when we had returned from dinner the board was there, but on top of the mattress with just a sheet over it. Maurice and I had properly positioned it under the mattress. Prior to leaving for Foshan today, we placed Mrs. Boehm's two mammouth bags on the adjacent bed for ease of packing. She just discovered the board again on top of the mattress with the big bags on top of it. We spend considerable time and laughter trying to analyze the reasoning behind the bed arrangements.

The morning of the 15th brings sad farewells, especially with Mr. Chou and Mrs. Chang. Mrs. Boehm and Mrs. Chang have become very close during our sixteen days in China; and for Mr. Chou it is an emotional departure, as it is for us. In a spontaneous gesture of affection, Mrs. Boehm removes the cashmere scarf which she wore throughout China and wraps it around Mrs. Chang's neck. Although we are not to give gifts to our friends individually, all recognize this is different, special, and nod with their approvals with smiling faces.

These gracious, hospitable people gave us a degree of kindness and friendship rarely experienced. They tended to our every need and took care of all planning and details during our trip—arranging transportation, having our luggage moved, guiding us during our shopping sprees, interpreting at an exhaustive pace for three very loquacious people, seeing to our meals and other comforts, and dozens of small gestures that make us feel we were their honored guests.

The people of the Friendship Association were superb hosts

and representatives everywhere we went. Their primary goal of making lasting friends of foreign guests who visit China is being attained admirably. We hope that when some of their members come to America, as they will in time, their equivalent host organization will return their kindnesses in full measure.

Mr. Tan is to accompany us on the train to the border and will see to it that our passage through customs will be expedited without inspection. In addition he has arranged for a China Travel Service agent to meet us over the border for our final leg to Hong Kong.

The ultimate gesture of friendship occurs just before we depart the Guest Hotel. Professor Kao hands Mrs. Boehm a package wrapped in plastic. It's the precious pug clay from Ching-te-Chen, about three pounds of it. Somehow arrangements were made on the 11th of December to drive it from the inaccessible porcelain center to Nanchang, there placed on a plane to Canton to reach us before our departure three days later. We are anxious to take it to our studios, shape it into a cup and saucer, add acid-etch gold decoration, and return the finished pieces to our friends in Ching-te-Chen. Soon after our return home, this was done. The clay fulfilled all our expectations.

We leave Canton on the 8:20 a.m. train which arrives at Shum chun (the border town) at 10.05. After seeing us through customs, Mr. Tan walks us to the small bridge separating China from Hong Kong. Our luggage automatically is transferred. The Hong Kong border town is Lo Wu. At 11:00 we board another train for the final 22-mile run to Kowloon, arriving at the Peninsula Hotel at 12:30.

CHAPTER XIII

Reflections

OUR TRIP to China is ended. The days passed so quickly. It will take weeks, maybe months for the full meaning and impact of the trip to resolve itself in our minds. Talking about the trip with friends and family will help sort it all out. Writing about it daily has forced us to crystallize some of our thoughts and feelings as we went.

In one subject area, ceramics, we feel secure and confident in our appraisals. As to the current status of quality and skill levels in China, they are equal to the world's finest. In some cases they may be superior; but the emphasis is primarily on the simpler, mass-produced subjects. This is because of the tremendous demand for their tablewares and average lines, both at home and in the world market; and secondly, their interest in obtaining foreign exchange.

So long as these conditions persist, it is doubtful more attention will be given to the fine art ceramics. From what we could ascertain, only about 5% of exports (exports account for 60% to 80% of total production) are from fine arts factories. Yet we are encouraged to see that the outstanding skill and artistic excellence are not being snuffed out. The Chinese are justly proud of their best work and recognize its importance promotionally and artistically.

The Ching-te-Chen Fine Arts Factory is the most outstanding in China for its beautiful thin, white porcelain body and its hand-painted decorative vases, urns, tablewares and coffee and tea sets. The incomparable pure white clays enjoy a strength which supports the thinness of an eggshell or light bulb and a startling translucency. Glazes are water-clear and brilliant.

Other clays used in Ching-te-Chen and Tangshan are similar in their properties to our Trenton materials. No bone is used in Chinese porcelains. No doubt the addition of calcined ox bone beginning with Thomas Frye of Bow in England (about 1749) was one of many attempts by the West to duplicate the whiteness of fine Chinese bodies.

Figurines and sculptures reflect the mass-production emphasis, as well as the current Chinese determination not to give great importance to traditional and pre-revolutionary work, and the firm policy of using art as a vehicle for political themes and messages. The Foshan stoneware figures are the best we saw.

The future potential of Chinese exports seems unlimited. The centers we visited all have increased production five to eight times since the late 1950s. As indicated before, current production probably approximates half a billion pieces a year. Without increasing the rate of output, the Chinese can be expected to double total production in five years to an annual production of about a billion pieces. With additional technical installations (in which the Chinese have intense interest), the total could be higher.

The friendship and sincerity we felt throughout China cannot be expressed adequately. The people-to-people relationship is always emphasized. Other than the revered Chairman Mao, leaders of either country rarely were mentioned. Several of our new friends made a point of saying that American and Chinese friendship will continue to grow regardless of the parties and persons in position of power and authority; that no American elected official can reverse this trend. The most often mentioned American is former President Nixon. In spite of the problem of Watergate, the Chinese still hold him in high esteem for having opened the door to friendship between our two countries.

Before our trip to China we heard many opinions about the practical reasons behind the P.R.C.'s invitation to Mrs. Boehm. Most felt the Chinese primarily were interested in learning from us detailed information about our production techniques, marketing, pricing, and distribution, and obtaining an analysis of their current production and design; and, conversely, that they would not divulge the same to us. All were way off the mark. Our hosts everywhere opened their doors and hearts to us and, if anything, we were somewhat embarrassed that we may never respond in full as it is doubtful any of them ever will have an opportunity to visit our studios. We now know that the primary purpose of the invitation was for a much more important reason: friendship. That is why we were the guests of the Chinese People's Association for Friendship with Foreign Countries.

A final summation about the conditions and lifestyle of China. Travel and accommodations, while always graciously offered anywhere in China, are better in the larger cities. By no means is China yet prepared to receive large numbers of foreign travelers; but they are building hotels at a rapid rate and are anxious to provide Western comforts for visiting friends. Hotels in smaller cities do not always have heat or hot water. Overall we found travel conditions a great deal better than we had been told to expect.

In keeping with Chairman Mao's Communist principles of equality and of identification with the workers, clothing design and style follow a male military concept. Greens, blues, blacks and grays predominate and we saw no women in skirts or dresses. Only occasionally did we see adult variations in color. Yet the very young children are gaily dressed as in Western countries. Nothing is spared to provide the youngest with colorful and happy surroundings. There will be time enough to teach them the disciplines and responsibilities of growing up in a Communist state.

Cuisine throughout China is excellent. Having been devotees of good oriental cooking before, we ogled, savored and enthusiastically enjoyed every new eating experience. Our eagerness to satisfy our palates and hosts, however, has cost us. We have all had a substantial weight gain.

English-speaking peoples will face a decreasing number of communication problems when in China. English is the number one foreign language in their schools. All over China we met young people who speak it fluently.

There are no difficulties sending cables; and the efficiency and clarity of overseas calls really impressed us. We placed four calls to the States. Each came through almost exactly on the minute requested.

Integrity and honesty are two of the guideposts of Mao's teachings, by-products of the everpresent themes of self-reliance and Chinese pride. And from what we observed, there is little, if any, crime or vice in China. We felt secure everywhere of our persons and possessions. We were jolted back to reality when we returned from China to Hong Kong and were forewarned by the Chinese travel agent to lock our luggage and hotel rooms.

Living conditions in China still are quite low by U.S. standards. But they differ from the past in that everyone now has enough to eat and wear, education is being made available throughout the country, and there is a sense of purpose and organization. The peasant and his agriculture are elevated to a place of honor in this agrarian economy (agriculture employs 85% of the people). And by having the administrators and intellectuals join in the fields periodically (six months of every two years), farming has acquired a heightened dignity.

Few modern conveniences and little technology have yet reached the rural areas. Man and his water buffalo, horses and mules carry on as they have for centuries. The number of jobs in a given area or project depends upon the number of people. There is an exaggerated division of labor which puts everyone to work who is able, young and old, male and female. One wonders if an increasing technology is compatible with a super-abundance of labor. What would be done with the displaced workers? Just paving a dirt road for ten miles would put a few hundred people out of work. Although the Chinese constantly speak of the need for Western technology, its broad implementation would have to be a slow and gradual process.

The unique Chinese political mind and process are not always easy for us to understand. Leadership roles of the young and old are somewhat reversed. A figure such as Confucius, whose doctrines influenced more than 2,000 years of Chinese life, is completely discredited and labeled an oppressor of the people. Former strong men like Liu Shao-chi and Lin Piao are branded revisionists and thrown into disgrace. Young Red Guards periodically remove and shame administrators and intellectuals who might be sliding into self-service and individual gain. Convulsions recur in the continuing Chinese Cultural Revolution. And yet progress, discipline, motivation, pride and a singleness of purpose are seen everywhere in China. How did all this happen in so short a period of time and what is the force behind it?

The answer largely can be found in Chairman Mao's teachings. His litany of equality among men, the State serving the people, and communal ownership of land and property are powerful and magnetic ideas to a people whose overwhelming numbers languished hopelessly in poverty under generations of feudalism.

Confucianism is the antithesis of Communism. It defines codes of conduct for different classes from rulers to vassals; obedience to authority; respect for higher offices and for ritual; reverence for the status quo. All imply a structured society, a caste or class system, not a classless people with equality as envisioned by Mao.

In order to fulfill his Marxist doctrine in the face of thousands of years of feudal history and tradition, Mao proposes a continuing struggle against bourgeois thinking and practices. Literature, art, music, education: all must be constantly employed in the struggle. Periodic convulsions are necessary to "shake out, identify and rehabilitate new revisionists."

Liu Shao-chi was removed because he wanted to create a new class of party officials, experts, intellectuals and soldiers with more power and wealth than the peasants.

Lin Piao, it is said, had conspired to assassinate Mao after which he would have taken control and set up a ruling class of officials in which he would have assumed the role of a dictator. Maoists refer to Lin Piao as a crypto-Confucian.

The continuing campaign to criticize Liu Shao-chi, Lin Piao, Confucius, and other forms of government is intended to root out remaining revisionist and Confucianist thinking in Chinese minds. And it hopes simultaneously to firmly implant the idea that no one leader or group of leaders can replace Mao when he dies. Only the millions of Chinese together can.

The tools Mao employs, to keep his 850 million people on the road toward classless Communism, are the youth. His vision, as expressed in his teachings, is wide, simple and penetrating. Young minds, uncluttered with the problems of adulthood and full of innocence and idealism, grasp it fervently.

There are about 150 million between the ages of twelve and twenty-one representing China's first partially-educated peasantry. Another 150 million are between twenty-one and thirty-five. Over half the Chinese population has been brought up in the permeating glare of Maoism.

As described earlier, the children are different from those of other countries. Other than the very young, they have a serious, determined mien. They speak and act in simplistic, direct ways. There is no question in their minds that the world is theirs, that Maoist Communism is inevitable for the world's poor people. Ten and eleven-year-olds are confident and poised. The action of bowing by the old people and their extreme politeness are not understood by these children. To them everyone is equal and all should be treated the same.

So the young have taken over the country and are Mao's staunch disciples. In 1966 Mao realized that revisionists were gradually consolidating positions of power. He called on the young Red Guard and about twelve million rallied around him and shouted and shamed the enemies out of power. They turned the people back toward Maoism.

With the energy of youth they practice as well as espouse equality, self-reliance, cooperation, respect for agriculture and all of the other tenets of Mao. They are filled with Maoist fraternity, courage and morality. School assignments are zealously studied. Vocational work seems almost sacred. Bright students and workers help their slower colleagues. When not in school little Red soldiers look for ways to help others. They run errands, care for the youngest, clean the streets, help the ill and elderly, build irrigation ditches and dikes, and flock to the fields to help with the harvests.

And they are politically active, clustering together studying Mao's writings, exchanging thoughts on how to imbue the older generations with their deep loyalties and beliefs. Thousands go into the towns and villages to educate the peasants and to elicit support for the revolution.

Whatever one's feelings about Mao's form of Communism, it must be granted that it appears to be working for the Chinese people. Whether it will continue to work still remains to be seen. The Chinese speak of increasing the living standards of their people. Yet economic prosperity may be incompatible with classless Communism. What of the aggressive, educated, activist children once they become men and women, mothers and fathers? Will their desires for a more expressive, creative life for their children dim their revolutionary spirit? Will their maturing appetites turn them more toward spiritual and material comforts of the mind and body? It will be fascinating to observe the answers to these and other questions as the transition of China continues in the post-Mao period.

Bibliography

Buerdeley, Cecile and Michel. *A Connoisseur's Guide to Chinese Ceramics*. New York: Harper & Row, Inc., 1974.

Cosentino, Frank J. *Boehm's Birds: The Porcelain Art of Edward Marshall Boehm*. New York: Frederick Fell, Inc., 1960.

Cosentino, Frank J. *Edward Marshall Boehm, 1913—1969*. Trenton, New Jersey: Edward Marshall Boehm, Inc., 1970.

Cox, Warren E. *The Book of Pottery and Porcelain*. New York: Crown Publishers, 1944.

Howe, James L., Jr. *Kintechin*. Lexington, Virginia: James L. Howe, Jr., Publisher, 1924.

Pope, John A. *The Frick Collection—Oriental Porcelains*. New York: The Frick Collection Publishers, 1974.